"Eloquent and enthralling . . . [*Pageboy*] is an intense, emotional read, delivered in image-drenched prose. 'Let me just exist with you,' he writes, 'happier than ever.' Reading those words nearly made me cry. Page's plea is small. It also feels very big."

—*The Washington Post*

"Powerful." —*The New York Times Book Review*

"Vivid . . . Moving . . . Juicy." —Tonya Mosley, NPR's *Fresh Air*

"Elliot Page's buzzy memoir is a brutally honest story of survival . . . piec[ing] together childhood flashbacks, haunting memories of Hollywood policing his queerness, visceral meditations on gender dysphoria, and ecstatic recollections of gender euphoria."

—*Time* ("The 100 Must-Read Books of 2023")

"*Pageboy* is like listening to a friend. . . . Now is an excellent time to read this humanizing and well-written memoir."

—Associated Press

"An alternately whimsical and genuinely meaningful experience."
—*Vogue* ("The Best LGBTQ+ Books of 2023 (So Far)")

"A lyrical story about queer becoming and gender discovery."
—*Harper's Bazaar* ("The Best Queer Reads of 2023")

"The emergence of our true selves is all of our life's work. *Pageboy* helps chart the course." —Jamie Lee Curtis

"Searing, deeply moving, and incredibly poignant . . . This isn't simply a book on what it means to be trans, it's about what it means to be human." —Alok Vaid-Menon

"Raw, harrowing, and often heartbreaking to read . . . Page's book arrives, as if on cue, in a moment when the trans community is facing even more danger than when he started writing it just over a year ago." —*Los Angeles Times*

"A beautiful, compelling gut punch of a book."
—Thomas Page McBee, award-winning author of *Amateur*

"At its heart [*Pageboy*] is the story of his transitioning. . . . He writes, rather beautifully, about gender dysphoria, top surgery, and finally finding himself. But the book is so much more than a tale of transition. *Pageboy* is a modern-day *Hollywood Babylon*, written by a sensitive soul." —*The Guardian*

"It's this prevailing sense of assurance and confidence in Page's voice that makes one of the year's most anticipated titles worth the wait."
—*Esquire* ("The 20 Best LGBTQ Books of 2023 (So Far)")

"An affecting and timely memoir." —*Kirkus Reviews*

"This is not just a story of growing up, of becoming, of transforming and surviving, but one of choosing to live and to fight for that life, even when the costs are higher than anyone could possibly imagine."
—*Autostraddle*

"*Pageboy* is an affirming declaration of self-acceptance that is more than likely to inspire and comfort others seeking solace."
—*Observer*

"An intimate, vulnerable, and poetic coming-into-self story."
—*Book Riot*

"Page's compassion-inducing account feels vital. . . . Heartfelt and courageous in its honesty." —*i* (UK)

"Singular." —*The Daily Telegraph* (UK)

"A profoundly talented writer . . . It is a love story of sorts in which the greatest love turns out to be Page's alignment with his truest self." —Elizabeth Day, author of *How to Fail*

PAGEBOY

—

A Memoir

ELLIOT PAGE

FLATIRON
BOOKS
NEW YORK

www.flatironbooks.com

An extension of this copyright page appears on page 269.

Designed by Donna Sinisgalli Noetzel

The Library of Congress has cataloged the hardcover edition as follows:

Names: Page, Elliot, 1987– author.
Title: Pageboy : a memoir / Elliot Page.
Description: First edition. | New York : Flatiron Books, 2023.
Identifiers: LCCN 2022061625 | ISBN 9781250878359 (hardcover) |
    ISBN 9781250291516 (signed) | ISBN 9781250878366 (ebook)
Subjects: LCSH: Page, Elliot, 1987– | Actors—Canada—Biography. |
    Actors—United States—Biography. | Transgender men—Canada—
    Biography. | LCGFT: Autobiographies.
Classification: LCC PN2308.P34 A3 2023 | DDC 791.4302/8092 [B]—
    dc23/eng/20230302
LC record available at https://lccn.loc.gov/2022061625

ISBN 978-1-250-87837-3 (trade paperback)

Our books may be purchased in bulk for promotional, educational, or business use. Please contact your local bookseller or the Macmillan Corporate and Premium Sales Department at 1-800-221-7945, extension 5442, or by email at MacmillanSpecialMarkets@macmillan.com.

First Flatiron Books Paperback Edition: 2024

10 9 8 7 6 5 4 3 2 1

To all those who came before

Contents

x   Contents

Author's Note

Writing a book has come up a few times over the years, but it never felt right and, quite frankly, it didn't feel possible. I could barely sit down, let alone be still long enough to complete such a task. My brain's energy was being wasted, a ceaseless drip attempting to conceal and control my discomfort. But now is different. New. At last, I can sit with myself, in this body, present—typing for hours, my dog, Mo, lounging in the sun, my back straighter, my mind quieter. This previously unimaginable contentment wouldn't have arrived without the health care I've received, and as attacks against gender-affirming care increase, along with efforts to silence us, it feels like the right time to put words on a page.

So here I am, grateful and terrified, writing directly to you. Trans people face increasing physical violence, and our humanity is regularly "debated" in the media. And, when we are given the opportunity to tell our stories ourselves, queer narratives are all too often picked apart or, worse, universalized—one person becomes a stand-in for all. There are an infinite number of ways to be queer and trans, and my story speaks to only one. As I say later in these pages, we are all but a speck in this universe, and I hope that in speaking my truth I have added yet another speck to dispel the constant misinformation around queer and trans lives. If you haven't already, I urge you to seek out many other vast and varying narratives from LGBTQ+ writers, activists, and individuals. The movement for trans liberation affects us all. We all experience gender joyfully and oppressively in different ways. As Leslie Feinberg writes in *Trans Liberation,* "This movement will give you more room to breathe—to be yourself. To discover on a deeper level what it means to be yourself."

In writing this story, I have remembered each moment to the best of my ability. When I could not remember details, I reached out to others who shared those experiences to gain more clarity. A few names have been changed and some other specifics have been altered when necessary to protect the identity of certain people. At certain points I've referred to myself using my previous name and pronouns. This is a choice that felt right to me, occasionally, when talking about my past self, but it's not an invitation for anyone to do the same. It's also important to note that while, in my life, gender and sexuality have been in constant conversation, these are two separate things. Coming out as queer was a wholly different experience from coming out as trans, and who I am evolved as I freed myself from the expectations of others. These memories shape a nonlinear narrative, because queerness is intrinsically nonlinear, journeys that bend and wind. Two steps forward, one step back. I've spent much of my life chipping away toward the truth, while terrified to cause a collapse. This is reflected on the page intentionally. In many ways, this book is the story of my untangling.

The act of writing, reading, and sharing the multitude of our experiences is an important step in standing up to those who wish to silence us. I've nothing new or profound to say, nothing that hasn't been said before, but I know books have helped me, saved me even, so perhaps this can help someone feel less alone, seen, no matter who they are or what journey they are on. Thank you for wanting to read about mine.

This world has many ends and beginnings

A cycle ends, will something remain?

Maybe a spark once so bright will bloom again.

—BEVERLY GLENN-COPELAND,
"A SONG AND MANY MOONS"

1

PAULA

———

I met Paula when I was twenty. Sitting on our friend's couch, eating raw almonds with her knees to her chest, she introduced herself, "I'm Paula." The sound of her voice radiated warmth, a kindness. It wasn't so much that her eyes lit up but that they found you. I could feel her looking.

We went to Reflections. It was the first time I had been to a gay bar and would be my last for a long time. I was a miserable flirter. Flirting when I didn't mean to and not when I wanted to. We stood close, but not too close. The air so thick, I was swimming in it.

That summer we took a friend's boat to an empty island to camp. We did mushrooms around fires and cooked salmon wrapped in tinfoil. Stars pulsating, reaching, as if forming sentences. Mushrooms always made me cry, but she loved them, eventually my anxious tears turned to joy. I envied the self-assurance in her body. We danced on the beach. A guitar was being strummed, we took turns playing shitty covers.

I had just returned from a monthlong trip in Eastern Europe, backpacking with my childhood best friend, Mark. We began in

Prague and took the train to Vienna, Budapest, Belgrade, and Bucharest. We stayed in hostels, except for one day in Bucharest when Mark was so ill that we got a hotel room with air-conditioning. I bought individually wrapped cheese slices from the store and put them in the small freezer of the small hotel room's small fridge. We waited as they became cold, and I pressed damp cloths on the back of his neck and along his spine. When the cheese slices were frozen I placed them all over Mark's body, and that seemed to help a bit. The room had a Jacuzzi, and we sat in it without filling it up and flipped through the television channels, landing on a porno that incidentally also took place in a Jacuzzi. Mark ate the cheese.

This was before smartphones. Navigating trains, hostels, men, all with one guidebook. We would go to internet cafés to send a message home. "Hey, we are alive." I would email Paula, yearning for her. I thought about her incessantly—while we railed through Austria, looking at a sea of sunflowers; while I drank blueberry beer in a basement in Belgrade, lips purple, head spinning, like the last time we kissed, which was the first time; on a twelve-hour train ride from Belgrade to Bucharest during one of the worst heat waves in decades. Mark and I lay next to each other on the same bunk, window down with our heads as close to the opening as we could manage. There was no air-conditioning, and we had no water. We listened to Cat Power through shared earphones and sipped absinthe. *Are you listening to it at the same time? The CD I made you?* I wondered, almost saying the words out loud. I watched the night pass by, the Serbian landscape, rural, motionless with its sparse, fleeting lights. I thought of Paula.

That time at Reflections was new for me, being in a queer space and being present, enjoying it. Shame had been drilled into my bones since I was my tiniest self, and I struggled to rid my body of that old toxic and erosive marrow. But there was a joy in the room, it lifted me, forced a reaction in the jaw, an uncontrolled, steady smile. Dancing, sweat dripping down my back, down my chest. I watched Paula's hair twist and bounce as she moved effortlessly, chaotic but controlled, sensual and strong. I would catch her looking at me, or was it the other way around? We wanted to be caught. Deer in the headlights. Startled, but not breaking.

"Can I kiss you?" I asked, jolted by my boldness, as if it came from somewhere else, powered by the electronic music perhaps, a circuit of release, of demanding you leave your repression at the door.

And then I did. In a queer bar. In front of everyone around us. I was coming to understand what all those poems were about, what all the fuss was. Everything was cold before, motionless, emotionless. Any woman I had loved hadn't loved me back, and the one who maybe had, loved me the wrong way.

But here I was, on a dance floor with a woman who wanted to kiss me and the antagonizing, cruel voice that flooded my head whenever I felt desire was silent. Maybe for a second, I could allow myself pleasure. We leaned in so our lips brushed, the tips of our tongues barely touching, testing, sending shocks through my limbs. We stared at each other, a quiet knowing.

Here I was on the precipice. Getting closer to my desires, my dreams, me, without the unbearable weight of the self-disgust I'd carried for so long. But a lot can change in a few months. And in a few months, *Juno* would premiere.

SEXUALITY SWEEPSTAKES

———

THE ELLEN PAGE SEXUALITY SWEEPSTAKES—I read the headline, color draining from my face. It was an article by Michael Musto in *The Village Voice* during the peak of *Juno*'s success. I scanned the rest of the piece. Among his speculation about a twenty-year-old's sexuality, Michael included, "I mean, come on already, is she??? You know, Lebanese! She certainly dresses like a, you know, tomboy . . . Let's put the dykey pieces together. Is Juno a you know?"

I had been thrust into the spotlight overnight, but I'd already been called a dyke many times while growing up in Canada. The bullying had taken on a new tone in high school, from little quips by the popular girls to the relatively dramatic display of being physically forced into the boys' bathroom. Pushed in, nostrils distorted by that foreign, urinal smell, I waited a moment, listening for their glee to dissipate, to soften with distance—only to exit and have the stern, narrow face of my English teacher glaring directly at me: "To the office!" I apologized. I didn't say I was pushed in.

Not long before the bullying amped up, I had been rooming with a girl named Fiona in the St. Francis Xavier University dorm for a soccer tournament. Saint FX is located in Antigonish, a town on the tip of northwest Nova Scotia, just a skip and a jump from Cape Breton. It hosts the oldest ongoing Highland games outside Scotland. *Nova Scotia* is Latin for "New Scotland," but the land it's on was originally named Mi'kma'ki. The Mi'kmaq have lived here for over ten thousand years.

I can still remember the sound of Fiona's laugh. I could hear it above any other noise, through all the static, penetrating my ears, swelling inside my body. I wanted to be near her, I wanted her to want me. I was a right-wing midfielder; speedy, small but scrappy. She was a sweeper, the last line of our team's defense and cocaptain with our center midfielder. She was a natural leader, commanding but kind. She had our backs. I loved watching her kick the ball—strong, fluid, and with a confidence I envied. I was crushing.

We lay in hard beds on either side of the room, the walls lined with dark, cheap wood. I looked at the ceiling and inhaled deeply, would I keep it in or let it out? The sensation was preternatural, as if I was spying on a potential future.

"I think I may be bisexual." I said this seemingly out of nowhere, having never conveyed anything like this to anyone.

"No you are not," she responded immediately, a sharp reflex, giggling after she said it.

This time, the sound of her laughter was harsh and cutting. Still, I wanted to laugh with her, *I mean being queer is funny and bad right?* The word "homosexuality" simply uttered in health class would give way to a cacophony of snickering. All the sitcoms I watched when I went home from school reinforced this. Whenever a joke was made, or I made one, it stuck; shit in the treads of my shoes. A spotlight moving stage right to stage left. I would tap-dance around it. Like a wet dog, I'd scramble to shake it off, to shake it out.

I can't remember what was said after, just the echoing laughter and the hard surface of the stiff bed.

Unable to sleep, I snuck out into the fluorescent hallway around 5:00 A.M. I sat on the floor to read. Kurt Vonnegut was the first writer I ever really liked, *thumbing the nose at You Know Who*. I was reading *Mother Night*, a novel of moral ambiguity. "We are what we pretend to be, so we must be careful about what we pretend to be," Vonnegut wrote. Sitting in the hall alone, I chewed on these words. Shame, with its steady swing, oscillated through my body. Something had slipped through my fingers. There was no catching it. I waited for the sun to rise.

We all ate breakfast together in the common area. There were Tim Hortons bagels and a large bag of oranges brought by a parent. The adults looked on, drinking their coffees. I ate silently. I didn't know how to look at Fiona and figured it was best to avoid the situation. I grabbed my shin pads, intending to get to the field early and warm up for the game.

"Dyke." The word smacked me across the face, said through that fiendish smirk I would come to know so well. As if gloating: *Ha, I'm nothing like you.* It came from a popular friend of Fiona's. And it stung. An isolated pain, a blink of language, but really, it's permanent.

Things changed after that. Something had been severed. I could sense the whispers, a shift in energy, the speculation. Perhaps it was good? That dangling tooth needed to be ripped out.

A few months later, my father and I were visiting my grandmother in Lockeport, Nova Scotia, a small fishing village with a population of just over five hundred located on the south shore of the province.

Fishing boats line the harbor, strung along the long pier, colors like Christmas lights. Worn yellow, a faded red, various shades of blue. A Nova Scotia postcard.

When I was a kid, my father would take me to Lockeport on July 1, a holiday in my homeland called Canada Day. Think July Fourth, but with less independence from the Crown, more "Canada's birthday." As a white kid growing up in Nova Scotia, I'd no clue about our history or our present. I was not taught it, the degree of our genocidal roots, the systemic racism, the segregation.

I thought Canada Day was all about fireworks, a parade, strawberry shortcake in the church basement, and, my favorite event on July 1, the "grease pole." A long, thin log was laid down on the pier, protruding out over the harbor, with a long drop to the water. Lard has been rubbed all over the hard wood, smothering it. On the far end, stretching out over the ocean, is a whack of cash held down by a chunk of lard that competitors attempt to retrieve. There are only two strategies really. One, on the stomach, slow, a small slither forward, slow again. This typically fails. Instead, the key seemed to be gliding out with as much speed as possible, swiping off as much money as you could while beginning your descent toward the frigid Atlantic. Emerging, you collect the fallen bills through the shock of the cold. Seagulls circle above, diving for the floating fat. No, I've never tried it.

My grandmother still lived in the house where my father grew up. A small two-story with three bedrooms and white siding. Behind it, forest, endless forest. Across the street was my grandfather's general store, Page's Store. It is still there, though I am not sure what it is called now. They added a gas pump.

The bedrooms upstairs were connected by a closet space that tunneled from one room to the other. As a kid, I'd escape into it, waltzing into an imagined dimension, the door so small, as if designed for me. I would pull the chain on the bare bulb, illuminating my assortment of treasures. It all felt very cinematic. I'd look through the boxes of bullets, inspecting them, eyes close like a jeweler, fascinated that something so minuscule could kill the bucks I would see jetting through the woods. Their stoic bodies barreling, seemingly too magnificent to crumple over such a tiny little thing.

"Dennis, what are you gonna do if Ellen's a dyke?" my grandmother asked my father as we all sat in her sunroom. Her voice that same sharp tone she used when saying racist things. In the Alanis Morissette version of irony, this was the same grandparent who had given me a bear with rainbows on its paws and ears when I was born. I was sixteen now and had recently shaved my head for a film. A Blue Jays game played, baseball was her favorite sport and Toronto her beloved team, or was it Boston? That was one of the last times I would see my grandmother before she passed. I wonder what she would think of her grandson now if she were still alive. I doubt she would choose rainbows anymore. Some people do change, though.

The success of *Juno* coincided with people in the industry telling me no one could know I was queer. That it wouldn't be good for me, that I should have options, to trust that this was for the best. So I put on the dresses and the makeup. I did the photo shoots. I kept Paula hidden. I was struggling with depression and having panic attacks so bad I would collapse. I could barely function. Numb and quiet, nails in my stomach, I was incapable of articulating the depth of pain I was in, especially because "my dreams were coming true," or at least that is what I was being told. I dismissed my feelings as dramatic, berated myself for being ungrateful. I felt too guilty to say I was hurting, incapacitated, that I didn't see a future.

I called my manager after reading the piece by Michael Musto, only to be met with a follow-up blog post detailing their phone conversation: "'It's not mean to wonder if someone's gay,' I shrieked, outraged." Sure, it is not mean to simply wonder if someone's gay. What *was* thoughtless and dangerous was writing something without any concern for a young queer person's journey.

Juno had premiered at the Toronto International Film Festival to a fervent response. I did not have a personal publicist at the time. I'd decided I could go it alone after a previous experience where an innocent teenage question—"Did you ever watch *Xena?*"—was met with "No, because I'm not a lesbian." I was glad to not be working with that publicist anymore—these comments emblematic of the Hollywood they warn you about. Plastic, empty, homophobic. Still, I wasn't prepared or experienced enough to navigate this new fame alone.

It is different growing up as an actor in Canada, especially when I did. Canada didn't have the glossy cover. We weren't so obsessed with being shiny. The insistence to mask up mostly came with *Juno.*

I was planning on wearing jeans and a western(ish) shirt to *Juno*'s world premiere. I thought it was a cool look, and it had a collar. *That's fancy, right?* I thought. When the Fox Searchlight publicity team learned about my outfit, they urgently took me to Holt Renfrew on Bloor Street, with a dramatic rushing that is characteristic of the Hollywood circulatory system. I suggested a suit. They said I should wear a dress and heels. After they discussed this with the director, he called me. He said he agreed with them, insisting that I play the part. Michael Cera rocked sneakers, slacks, and a collared shirt. He looked fancy to me. I wonder why they didn't take him to Holt Renfrew. I guess he had nothing to hide, he was approved. He fit the part.

Being made to feel that I was inadequate, erroneous, the little queer who needed to be tucked away while being celebrated for repudiating myself was a slippery slope I'd been sliding down since before I could remember. And like a film stuck to my skin, I couldn't wash it off. The compulsion to tear apart my flesh, a sort of scolding—I became as repulsed as them.

I was spending more and more time in Los Angeles. Press for *Juno,* meetings, "awards season," which is two actual seasons. Back in Nova Scotia, another publication investigated my sexuality, perhaps trying to win Michael Musto's "sexuality sweepstakes." *Frank,* a "magazine" that has been published out of Halifax since 1987, considered itself a satirical magazine but was actually more like a tabloid. I was in Santa Monica when my father called to tell me that I was on the cover, a photo of me from Sundance with a giant headline that read IS ELLEN PAGE GAY?

I spun out. In bed at a friend's guesthouse, I closed my wet eyes tight, tears soaking my cheeks—*please let this be a dream. Please.*

When I got back to Halifax, the magazine was everywhere. Always sitting in view at the grocery store, the gas station, the corner store . . . and there they all were, asking the question—*Is Ellen Page Gay?* Paula would flip them around. Hide them behind other magazines. Once she stole a bunch from a gas station in the South End.

The freedom I felt during my summer with Paula was coming to an end.

There was a photograph inside that included Paula. A small group of us at a party. I remember that night, a gathering at an apartment in one of the drab condo buildings that continue to overtake Halifax. The article speculated whether we were in a relationship or not, examining the rumors. Paula was still not out to her family. Staring at that picture, a realization: *a friend must have sent this to them.* I never knew who.

3

BOY

———

We matched online, my first time on a dating app, my first time dating as an out trans person. After eating dinner in the Meatpacking District, I hopped on the train to Midtown to meet up with Sara and her friends. I was nervous, but energized, these spontaneous adventures new to me.

The bar was tacky, but I liked it. Searching for her, my eyes landed on a group of women. They sat at a high table with stools, already a few drinks in. I hate tall stools, they don't work well with my short legs. The women greeted me kindly, welcoming me, pulling up another seat.

All of them were gorgeous, hovering around six feet. I was dubious about my match with Sara. Were they just tipsy, swiping through the app, bemused by my presence on it? The little trans guy. Did they flip through all the cis dudes, the hot record producers, pro athletes, doctors, and then pause on my photo—a moment of disgust or merriment or both?

I ordered a tequila soda on the rocks with lime. TVs played, remnants of food were scattered on the table. I downed my drink and ordered another.

"Nova Scotia," I said, responding to the obligatory "Where are you from?" "It's in Canada," I added.

"What? I thought it was in Scandinavia or something?" one of her pals responded.

I finished my second drink and popped out to smoke a joint. Sara followed.

"When did you know?" she asked as we stood outside, leaning against a wall. She loomed over me. For a brief moment, I wondered what she meant. This is something I'm asked frequently and not something I wish for during a casual night out. I'd experienced this inquiry as a queer woman, but as a trans guy it's perpetual. Code for—*I don't believe you*.

I knew when I was four years old. I went to the YMCA preschool in downtown Halifax, on South Park Street across from the Public Gardens. The building had a dark brick facade and has since been demolished and replaced. Primarily, I understood that I wasn't a girl. Not in a conscious sense but in a pure sense, uncontaminated. That sensation is one of my earliest and clearest memories.

The bathroom was down the hall from my preschool class. I would try to pee standing up, assuming this to be the better fit for me. I would press on my vagina, holding it, pinching and squeezing it, hoping I could aim. I befouled the stall, but the bathroom often smelled of urine anyway.

I was perplexed by my experience, severed from the other girls, twists in my stomach when I gazed at them. I remember one in particular, Jane. Her long brown hair, the way she could draw, her eyes focused and still with concentration. I was jealous of her artistic abilities. When I drew a person, limbs would protrude out of the head, arms like branches, thin lines for fingers. Little chicken legs with oversize sneakers. Jane, however, would draw a body, a stomach, a belly button. I was transfixed. My first crush, but I knew I was not like her.

"Can I be a boy?" I asked my mother at six years old.

We lived on Second Street at the time, having moved only a few minutes' walk from our previous attic apartment on Churchill Drive. A ground-level flat on a tree-lined street, it had two bedrooms, hardwood floors, and a lovely small living area with big windows. I'd sit in front of the TV for hours playing Sega Genesis— *Aladdin, NHL '94, Sonic the Hedgehog*—praying to God when my back was against the ropes, requiring the all-magnificent force to help me beat the game. There are no atheists in foxholes.

"No, hon, you can't, you're a girl," my mother responded. She paused, not moving her eyes from the dish towels she was methodically folding, before saying, "But you can do anything a boy can do." One by one, stacking them neatly in their place.

It reminded me of how she looked when ordering a Happy Meal for me at McDonald's. I insisted on the "boys' toy" every time—a delightful, congenial bribe. My mother's discomfort requesting the toy was palpable, releasing a sort of shy giggle, slivers of shame peering through. Often they gave the girls' one anyway.

At ten, people started addressing me as a boy. Having won a yearlong battle to cut my hair short, I started to get a "thanks, bud" when holding the door for someone at the Halifax Shopping Centre.

It was unfathomable to me that I wasn't a boy. I writhed in clothes that were even in the slightest bit feminine. Everyone around me saw a different person than I saw, so for much of my childhood I preferred to be alone. I played by myself extensively. "Private play," I called it.

"Mom, I'm going to have private play now," I'd say as I marched up the stairs to my room, closing the door behind me.

I loved action figures—Batman and Robin, Hook and Peter Pan, Luke Skywalker, two Barbies from Happy Meals whose hair I cut off. The "girl toy" making it into the bag, despite the "boy toy" request. I was a walking stereotype, just not in the way my mom wanted.

Disappearing into private play for hours, I'd build forts on my bunk bed. It was metal, bars lined the bottom of the top bunk, and I would hang blankets and towels, making rooms. A little kitchen, a miniature bedroom. Vanishing into intricate and impassioned narratives, danger lurked, I'd hang off the top bunk, as if dangling from a cliff, facing death, using all my might to pull myself up to safety.

Imagined romances bloomed. I would write love letters to my fake girlfriend from across the lava floor, always signing, *Love, Jason*. I would tell her about my adventures abroad, how I longed for her, cared for her, that I needed her in my arms.

Those were some of the best times of my life, traveling to another dimension where I was . . . me. And not just a boy but a man, a man who could fall in love and be loved back. Why do we lose that ability? To create a whole world? A bunk bed was a kingdom, I was a boy.

My imagination was a lifeline. It was where I felt the most unrestrained, unselfconscious, real. Not a visualization, far more natural. Not a wishing, but an understanding. When I was present with myself, I knew, without exception. I saw with startling clarity then. I miss that.

Private play was similar to acting, the sensation a sort of paradox. My reliance on my imagination has carried me through life. Perhaps

I've been chasing that feeling ever since. "Acting, finding a character, it is like being possessed," Samantha Morton once said. Later, when I was sixteen, her performance in Lynne Ramsay's *Morvern Callar* would become one of my greatest inspirations. The quietness, the subtlety, the power of silence.

Before my taste in cinema led me to films like *Ratcatcher* and *Movern Callar,* I was stuck on disaster films. I rented *Anaconda* on my eleventh birthday, not a disaster film, but close. Anna, a girl in my class, had come over for a sleepover. We took a cold, short walk from home, cutting across the boulevard to Isleville Street, the grass hard and frozen, crunching under our feet. The video store was in a small brick building. We moved through the aisles, assessing the covers. After the demise of VHS tapes and DVDs, it became a salon. After the salon, I am not sure. The building isn't there anymore.

We trudged back home, clutching our prize, eagerly waiting for J.Lo, Ice Cube, and Owen Wilson to face off with the world's largest and deadliest snake.

"They strike, wrap around you. Hold you tighter than your true love. And you get the privilege of hearing your bones break before the power of embrace causes your veins to explode."

All the boys liked Anna, including me. Friends since primary, we went to school together and played on the same soccer team, the Halifax City Celtics. She was defense, right wing typically. We'd play *Aladdin* for hours on Sega Genesis. We'd jump on her bed, singing to Aqua in unison.

> I'm a Barbie girl, in the Barbie world
> Life in plastic, it's fantastic
> You can brush my hair, undress me everywhere
> Imagination, life is your creation

I often dreamed of being Aladdin. But it wasn't for the rug, or the wishes, or the teeny monkey, but to know what it feels like to delicately touch a girl. A sparkle of romance. I remember sitting on a wall with Anna after school, waiting for my mother to pick me up. We sat with our legs dangling, looking down the quiet, leafy street. I slid my body closer to hers, barely touching, feeling the concrete scrape against me. I went to place my hand on her thigh.

"What are you doing?"

Her body recoiled as if grazed with a soldering iron. She didn't move after that, or speak, neither did I. Then her mom came and picked her up. Anna and I grew apart. She became very popular and I, as you can imagine, did not.

Still, it wasn't long before I started exploring sexually, but invariably with boys. My first kiss happened with a boy named Justin. He looked like a character from *The Lord of the Rings,* Cate Blanchett's elf son or something. He'd built a fort around his bed, and like little spelunkers we would crawl inside and make out to Kenny G. His family dog was small and white and the absolute worst, so mean. I would secretly feed the dog under the table, pinning my hopes on a soggy french fry, beseeching it to love, or at least tolerate, me.

We'd exchange notes at school. A new feeling, a flutter in my lower back, how did a little piece of paper with a few sentences alter me this way? Risky and exhilarating, it added a poetry to the days, transcending the mundane. Maybe not exactly right, but a path I couldn't stop walking down. A teacher intercepted one note,

Meet me in the corner of the backfield and I'll give you another massage.

My cheeks burned with embarrassment, frozen, but Justin, being a goddamn genius, said that he meant to write "message," but spelled it incorrectly. The teacher bought it.

I was with Justin the first time I was called a faggot. We were huddled in the trees of Fort Needham Memorial Park. The location burned in my memory. Fort Needham was established during the American Revolutionary War. It looked out over what is now Halifax's North End, where I grew up. Now, a bell tower stands atop the hill, built in remembrance of the Halifax Explosion. A major disaster forgotten by most of the world, but that quite literally shaped the entire landscape of my childhood, with evidence everywhere I turned.

The Halifax Explosion on December 6, 1917, involved a Norwegian relief ship, the *Imo,* and a French munitions ship, the *Mont-Blanc,* which contained 250 tonnes of TNT, 62 tonnes of guncotton, 246 tonnes of benzol, and 2,366 tonnes of picric acid. The cargo weighed six million pounds. Nineteen times the weight of the Statue of Liberty.

As detailed in John U. Bacon's book *The Great Halifax Explosion,* ships in Halifax Harbour transporting ammunition to Europe typically flew a red flag to signify the contents, but due to the threat of German U-boats outside the harbor, on its arrival the *Mont-Blanc* did not. Only five people in the city knew what was on that ship. As the *Mont-Blanc* discreetly made its way into Halifax Harbour at dawn, the *Imo* was gearing up for its voyage. The *Imo* had been delayed a day, waiting for a late coal shipment, and its captain now ventured out, irate from the lost time. He sped along the incorrect side as he approached the narrowest part of the harbor. A game of chicken commenced. One captain made the last-minute decision to turn. So did the other, and they collided.

People rushed toward the harbor and their windows as giant

smoke clouds rose, unaware of the *Mont-Blanc*'s contents. The ship burned for nearly twenty minutes and then detonated, leveling the entirety of the North End, more than 2.5 square kilometers destroyed. Over fifteen hundred people died instantly, left limbless, clothes ripped from their bodies. Vaporized. The force of the explosion caused a thirty-five-foot tsunami, sucking out bodies that would never be found. The blast was so extreme it was studied during the Manhattan Project to create the atomic bomb, a fact kept secret for decades.

Survivors screamed for help under the enormity of the destruction. Injured and dying. It was the morning, and woodstoves had been burning and the rubble ignited. The fire engulfed the ruins, people screamed for help, flames fast approaching. Survivors have said that their worst, tormenting memory is the sound of agony, the guttural screams coming from those trapped underneath. People were forced to flee, fire spreading. Parents leaving children, a lover leaving their soulmate. At least two thousand people died and over nine thousand were injured in what was the largest man-made explosion prior to the atomic bomb.

And that is where I sat kissing, decades later.

Together at the base of the conifers, an empty liquor bottle by our side, perhaps left by two other lovers. Touching. Kissing. Holding each other. We were two boys, and we looked like two boys.

"What are you, fucking faggots?" A group of teenagers were coming at us. Faggots. Faggots. Faggots.

They were bigger, menacing, cruel.

"Faggots. We are going to beat you up."

"I'm a girl," I told them.

"Oh then what are you, an alien?" They spat at Justin.

Something clicked, and we started to run. This wasn't going to be just words. Our legs flailing as we sprinted down the hill. Electricity in the gut. Every step a Hail Mary pass.

I fled toward my babysitter's house, thinking it a wiser choice than my own. There was no time to look over my shoulder, the voices kept coming. Miraculously, we made it to her porch. I could hear her Lhasa apso, Bubba, barking. The boys came to a stop. She came to the door, our panic clear. She looked to the group of boys, understanding coming to her eyes.

"Fuck off, you little shits!"

I can still see it, her yelling at them, it was rare to feel protected.

Growing up I was taught the *Mont-Blanc* explosion was an "accident," a "mistake." Two ships collided and one had explosives and that was that. It wasn't an accident, though—it was a consequence of war.

The explosion created thousands of orphans overnight. People were unhoused and hungry. St. Paul's Church served over ten thousand meals that month. My mother's father, who died when she was sixteen, was the minister there for years. St. Paul's evidently survived the blast, but the windows were shattered, along with all of the windows in all of Halifax, as many stood with their faces close, looking out at the rising smoke.

I imagine the carnage, the snow bloodred, an apocalyptic slaughter. Where did all that trauma go? Children, suddenly with no parents, walking in the midst of unspeakable devastation. What did queer people do after the tragedy? Those who lost secret lovers. The closeted grief.

4

ACTION FIGURES

———

My mom and I moved to the Hydrostone neighborhood in 1994 when I was just about to turn eight. It was developed after the blast that flattened the North End. The fire that had engulfed the rubble prompted the idea of hydrostones for the reconstruction, the only neighborhood like it in all of North America. Large, nonflammable slabs of concrete with crushed granite were used to build the row houses that make up the ten-blocks-long, one-block-wide neighborhood. A neighborhood shaped by devastation.

I loved growing up there, all the streets except for one had large boulevards, where kids would play and adults would lay out picnics. Back alleys snaked between the blocks, laundry waved its colors, chimes hung on the small back patios as cats lurked. I liked to roam the alleys by myself—a boy and his adventures.

When my mother bought her house, a two-bedroom with one bathroom, the neighborhood was still accessible for someone with her income—divorced, a single mom and teacher. She would pick me up from the after-school program in the early evening, asking me about my day, what I'd learned, what homework I had. I liked hearing about her stories, too, what happened in her classroom. One time she told me about a boy who stood on his desk and peed in defiance. Arriving home, I'd protest starting my homework as my mom ran a bath for me or started preparing dinner. She never did get a proper rest.

At bath time, I'd line up all of my various companions along the side of the tub and plead for my mother to be a judge for their diving competition. My arm in the air, holding Batman by the feet, I'd release him, and Bruce Wayne would enter the water, hopefully producing only a subtle splash to impress the judge.

"A seven!" my mom would say after my action figure had plunged into the depths.

"An eight!" After Peter Pan successfully slipped into the water.

"Yay!" I'd cheer, always secretly hoping Peter would win.

"Okay, hon, I've got to put supper on."

"One more! *Please,* Mom, *please!*"

"Okay, one more."

And I'd drop another.

When a winner was decided, I'd stand the figure proudly on the side of the tub as my mom hummed the Olympics theme, sometimes she would even light a match and hold it up like a torch.

The bath was also where I played out my rescue fantasies. I loved *Honey, I Shrunk the Kids* and was positively enamored with the daughter, Amy Szalinski. I couldn't take my eyes off her, her beauty, a sweetness in her voice, I loved how she cared for her younger brother.

In the bathtub, I was Russ Jr., the smoldering boy next door, rescuing Amy from drowning in the backyard-turned-oversize-jungle. Me as Russ Jr., panicked, but managing to maintain composure. Head under the water, I'd search, back up, flip around, under again, not giving up until I had rescued the one I love. Eventually getting her to safety, I would perform mouth-to-mouth on my hand, desperate for her to wake up. And only when she did could I let go. *I did it,* I'd think as I'd imagine myself flashing Russ Jr.'s signature half smile, that look I saw in his eyes.

My mom loved being a public school teacher, and she was an incredible one. She taught French for twenty-five years and English for eight, and I can't tell you the number of people who have said to me, "Madame Philpotts was the best teacher I ever had." Early on, I would help my mom set up her classroom at the end of the summer. Sticky tack-on posters. The months laid out, cutouts of the sun, clouds, snow. *Janvier, février, mars, avril.* I loved trips to the laminator, the smell of it, the way it wrapped something up, keeping it safe. The empty halls of the school were eerie, uncanny. Wandering through them had an unearthly quality, as if floating.

What was it like to spend your whole day in rooms stuffed with thirty elementary school students and then have to come home, make dinner, and judge your kid's fake diving competition? She'd been on her feet all day and now was crouched on the cold tile floor, I'm sure desperate for a comfy seat, warm food, and a cold beer, none of which were going to magically appear before her. These are important moments to remember. They aren't small.

On Saturdays, my mom would gather snacks and beverages and we'd settle together in the large beige chair that worked as a love seat. Turning on the television to CBC (Canadian Broadcasting Corporation), we'd prepare ourselves for *Hockey Night in Canada.* A Pepsi in my hand and an Alexander Keith's for my mom, we cheered and hollered with a large bag of ketchup chips wedged in between. The Toronto Maple Leafs was our team.

My mother let me exist as me in many ways when I was young,

when it was just us. It was on picture days, the rare church visit, weddings, recitals, Christmas parties, other special occasions when it wasn't just the two of us, that I had to wear a dress. A barrette in my hair with a baby-blue butterfly. I wanted to tear it out, taking my hair with it. I'd throw a fit, a feeling of betrayal spreading through me, as my mom tried to dress me. The sensation of tights squeezing my legs exacerbated all the discomforts that I couldn't yet put words to.

I didn't grow out of this "phase" when I was supposed to, and my mom's distaste for what I wore and whom I befriended grew. Masculine clothes and boys as friends should have been over, that whole tomboy thing—a label that never felt quite right to me, but it was what everyone called me so eventually it was what I called myself—a hazy memory. I should be turning into a young lady, my mother's idea of one at least.

"I just want what's best for you . . . I want to protect you . . . I don't want you to have a hard life." These sentiments would slide over me. What was best meant fitting neatly into our society's expectations. Staying inside the lines. The perfect heroine's journey preemptively and unknowingly written for me.

How would her family, friends, soccer parents, fellow teachers, and neighbors feel? Had she done something wrong? What if it was a sin? And whether it was conscious or not—*If I had to conform, why shouldn't you have to?*

I wonder about the magnitude of what my mom was unable to do and explore. How these confines affected her. Amid all of the untangling that's led me to me, no matter the difficulties or moments of distance, I've never doubted my mother's love for me. How lucky I am for that.

When I was little, my mom would take me out to Peggy's Cove, about a forty-five-minute drive from Halifax. Climbing on the rocks,

I'd pretend I was off in a distant land searching for treasure and mystical beings. I would examine the tide pools, looking for the life inside. My mom and I would talk on fake walkie-talkies, our fists held to our face. Click. Over. Click. Over.

Making sure to avoid the dark, wet boulders, we'd explore for ages, spotting little creatures scurrying under the rocks. When the waves were large it was positively thrilling. They'd smash against the shore with magnificent force, rising high and reaching toward the famous lighthouse, moments turned to postcards.

We'd end up at the parking lot outside of the restaurant that sits overlooking the cove. Seagulls circled above, waiting to pounce on scraps next to tourist buses. My mom loved the gingerbread there, so sometimes I got to have a treat.

Peggy's Cove afternoons with my mom are some of my best childhood memories. The ruggedness, that intense, unforgiving beauty. How present my mother and I were in each other's company. Our limbs stretching and reaching, feet searching for a spot to land, the salty, brisk chill of the Atlantic.

I love you. Over. Click.

I love you, too. Over. Click.

It is so sad that all the static had to get in the way as I aged. A dark rock on which to slip, suddenly appearing and taking us both down. That pure connection that went beyond appearance and expectations, both of us free in the moment—these are the memories I revisit.

In the winter, I looked forward to snow days. The suspense, sitting on the edge of my mom's bed next to the radio, wishing desperately, dreaming of snow forts and snowmen. I would close my eyes, listening to the CBC radio host recite a list of school cancellations, to the soothing voice.

Snow day mornings were absolute heaven. My mom and I had a ritual. I would sit in a purple plastic sled and she would pull me through the snow. The destination? Tim Hortons. Marching along, crunch, crunch, her boots sinking, everything covered in white, icicles like spears.

"I'll have a medium with double cream and just a pinch of sugar, not very much, thanks," I would mouth my mom's order at Tims in the mornings on the way to school while she leaned her head out the car window, neck reaching for the drive-thru speaker. For me, I liked the hot chocolate.

The sound of the little sled brushing the snow underneath, the steady glide through the barren landscape, offered tranquility, a sense of togetherness. Shut your eyes and you're flying through the universe.

5

ROUGHHOUSING

———

When the *Mont-Blanc* detonated, a gas fireball of coal, oil, cargo, ship parts, and humans catapulted two miles into the sky. Topping a thousand pounds, a piece of the *Mont-Blanc*'s anchor was found nearly two and a half miles away. The anchor site is on the cusp of the Regatta Point Walkway at the corner of Anchor Drive and Spinnaker Drive, a two-minute walk from where I grew up with my father.

I was under two when my parents divorced. They had been together for ten years, married for about eight of those, when my father first moved out into an apartment in downtown Halifax, where he lived until we moved to Spinnaker Drive when I was six. Mostly with my mother after the separation, I visited my father every other weekend or so. A thrilling vacation, the apartment building, directly across the street from the Halifax Harbour, had a pool . . . A POOL! You technically were not allowed to jump or dive, but we would in secret. One of us on the lookout for "cranky Cram," as my dad referred to the building supervisor.

The view of what the Mi'kmaq named K'jipuktuk, or "Great

Harbour," is now blocked by condos. But at five years old I could look out and study the boats and ships, my tiny brain struggling to deduce how objects that massive were smoothly gliding along the surface, how the masses of steel weren't just swallowed up. I'd watch them slowly make their way toward the Atlantic, floating beyond Georges Island. Named after a British king and smack-dab in the middle of the harbor, it was occupied by the British military in 1750. The island's fort became one of the most important naval bases for the British Empire in the eighteenth and nineteenth centuries. The intricate underground tunnel system sounded like something out of *The Goonies*. People spoke of ghosts, apparitions loitering, a result of executions, deaths in the prison camp and in the quarantine station on the island. Going to sleep, I selfishly prayed the ghosts couldn't swim.

My dad had recently started a graphic design business with a friend, Eric Wood. The Page & Wood office was inside the Brewery Market, a sprawling heritage building constructed in the 1800s out of granite and ironstone. Just a short walk from the apartment down Lower Water Street, it was mostly known for the farmers market every Saturday. In existence since 1983, the farmers market is where I've spent countless Saturday mornings weaving through the crowds, collecting produce, eating fresh cinnamon buns, listening to the fiddle echo through the main hall.

At the beginning, the office was quite small. My dad had a large, slanted white desk where he would brainstorm and sketch. At one point he got one of those golf-putting practice machines that shoots the ball back to you. Putting next to his desk, I'd make up stories—me, a cool professional golfer in one of those crisp collared shirts. Eighteenth hole, a putt for an eagle to win. I liked how men held the club with their hands, the way they adjusted their fingers, wiggled their feet, how they craned their wide necks to face the hole and looked back to the ball focused, then a steady, slight swing. I was flexible with the mulligans.

My dad, Dennis, was spending time with a woman named Linda, who would eventually become my stepmother. Linda and Dennis met when they worked in the same office. I think of my mother now, her husband leaving her for someone else. She was alone, taking care of the child and working full-time as a teacher. Then, I'd return all giddy and insensitive with stories about swimming, blabbering away about the new lady and her waterbed, no grasp of the hurt, the resentment. How that must have pierced her heart.

"It takes two," my mother says. "I had a role, too."

I've always found it strange that my mother and father had a baby. Me. Their relationship was already in trouble by the time I came along. I suppose gratitude is the course of action, but if I was not born, I'd have no perception of what I'd be missing, nor would anyone else miss me. This would suit me just fine. We are all micro specks, almost nothing in the grand scheme.

Linda lived in Clayton Park, an area in Halifax approximately a fifteen-minute drive from my father's. She had a condo in an apartment complex. Two stories, the kitchen, dining area, and living room on one floor and the pair of bedrooms and bathroom upstairs. Linda already had children from her previous marriage: Scott and Ashley. Scott was three and a half years older than me, Ashley another three years older than him. Their father was a teacher like my mom.

Scott and Ashley's room was rad. A wooden white bunk bed, Scott on the top, Ashley on the bottom. When I slept over, a small futon was rolled out on the floor. I was jealous of the top bunk, but my time would come. They had a TV *in their room* with a Nintendo, the original one that launched in 1985. Scott and I would play *Super Mario Bros.* and *Duck Hunt* for hours, staining the controllers with our ketchup chip–laced fingers.

Linda's room contained the aforementioned waterbed, still the only one I have ever witnessed in the flesh. My father and I would visit, Linda would make supper, typically I was off with Scott. My stepmom's "thing," shall we say, is cooking. She worked as a food stylist part-time, primping and prodding produce and meat, preparing the perfect turkey for a TV commercial or photo shoot. For one job, she had to make an exorbitant amount of ice cream, but it had to be fake so it would not melt. The breakfast table, island, and dining table were covered with a multitude of experiments and concoctions. What a cruel joke, fake ice cream.

The 1996 movie *Two If by Sea,* starring Sandra Bullock and Denis Leary, was set in New England but filmed in the towns Chester and Lunenburg, along the south shore of Nova Scotia. Linda styled a decadent dinner for a scene. Her work appearing in a Hollywood film had me buzzing, my heart aflutter for Sandra Bullock, my eight-year-old self not comprehending that I once again had a crush. Twenty years later I would have dinner with my friend Catherine Keener and Sandra at the famous Craig's in Beverly Hills. Sandra looked so cool, in jeans and a hip rocker T. She was nice, funny, and grounded, just as my eight-year-old self had imagined. Oh, these strange roads we travel.

Despite her supposed knack for cooking, I could not handle Linda's meals, incapable of digesting them. My father, stepbrother, and stepsister seemed to have no problem, enthusiastically moaning and complimenting. It felt as fake as the ice cream.

I hated food that wasn't simple. My mom's free time was minimal, she didn't have space in the day to put together lavish meals, with new tastes and smells. She was then teaching French at two or three schools on the outskirts of the city. Harrietsfield Elementary, William King Elementary, and Sambro Elementary, my favorite one. A small school, it is not far from Sambro Island's looming lighthouse, which is supposedly haunted. Legend has it that a Scot named Alexander Alexander (often referred to as Double Alexander) was stationed there, and when he left the island to buy supplies, he not only didn't retrieve the goods but also began a two-week drinking binge and then took his own life. People say Double Alex's ghost can be heard walking, screwing with the lights, and flushing toilets.

I wanted what my mother made, meat and potatoes, noodles with butter and steamed veggies. Linda's stir-fries hit my gag reflex, a sweetness I wasn't used to. Drinking copious amounts of milk, I'd be reprimanded for not eating. I'd chew and chew and chew and chew, as if I'd lost my ability to swallow, the muscle memory abruptly vanishing. As a toddler, I'd be left alone at the table when the others were done with a timer counting down. Tick. Tick. Tick. Tick. I had to eat it all before that screeching bell. This elongated chomping persisted as I aged, even her homemade pizza, a revelation that it wasn't just about flavor and aroma.

When I was six, we all moved in together. Dennis, Linda, Scott, Ashley, and I stood in the concrete foundation of the new development on Spinnaker Drive, surrounded by high, foreboding gray walls. Looking up, just sky, the treetops lining what would become the rear of the house, a small forest tucked up the hill from the back patio.

The tall, thin town house had four floors. A den and half bath in the basement. Living room, kitchen, and dining area on the second floor. On the third, my bedroom squeezed next to Scott's, a bathroom in the middle of the hall, with Dennis and Linda at the front of the house, their windows looking out to what the Mi'kmaq named Waygwalteech, meaning "salt water all the way up." A narrow section of Halifax Harbour, it outlines the west side of the Halifax Peninsula. Or, as it was renamed, the Northwest Arm.

My stepsister, Ashley, being the oldest, got the coolest room. The one on the top floor, a small attic space with a low, slanted ceiling. It would become my room when I returned from Toronto in my late teens, after grade eleven, to take an entire year off acting so that I could complete my final year of school in Halifax.

Directly across the street is Melville Cove, a small body of water that jets off the Arm and separates Regatta Point Walkway from the Armdale Yacht Club, which incidentally is also on an island with a centuries-old, supposedly haunted brick-and-iron prison where hundreds of people died, predominantly prisoners of war. Adjacent to the prison, on the sliver of a peninsula, Deadman's Island, there are almost two hundred unmarked graves of Americans who died in captivity during the War of 1812. A plaque reads:

> Go view the graves which prisoners fill
> Go count them on the rising hill
> No monumental marble shows
> Whose silent dust does there repose

I was obsessed with my new room. I was the first to leave a mark, a tiny stain on the wall waiting to be washed off. The color was my choice, and thankfully I was at an age where I could say what I *actually* wanted, versus putting on the dress for my birthday but not quite knowing why, like it was Halloween or something. I chose a dark blue, close to the deep shade of my stepbrother's. I tacked posters of Patrick Roy, Michael Jordan, and Joey McIntyre from New

Kids on the Block up on the wall. The bunk bed from Linda's old place, mine now. With both options available to me, I would switch. Sometimes top, sometimes bottom.

When Dennis and Linda moved in together, my time was split between households. Two weeks with my father, the first to the sixteenth of every month, and two weeks with my mother from the sixteenth to the first. Scott and Ashley did the same with their dad. At my dad's, my stepbrother and I played street hockey or "floor hockey" virtually every day after school, a game we invented in the small upstairs hallway where doors were goals, our hands the hockey sticks, the perfect snap of the wrist torpedoing the ball, jetting out a shin to make a sweet save.

I was into having an older brother. Scott was a jock, an excellent athlete, who went on to play Junior A hockey for years. A lot of my youth was spent in hockey rinks. I'd eat french fries and watch the brawls, transfixed by the bizarre, sanctioned fighting. When his friends came over I stayed close, that annoying kid brother who tags along. I loved how they dressed, how they smelled. The way they removed their T-shirts, reaching back over their shoulders, grabbing the fabric and pulling it up over their heads, revealing a torso, a dangling chain. I'd slink into Scott's room and dig out his cologne, not understanding the difference between a dab and a dollop. *Is this a magic potion?* I wondered. *Perhaps this would do it.* I snuck back out of his bedroom, the stench of a horny teenager trailing, as if I had plunged into an ocean of Old Spice.

Scott was very physical with me, as a lot of older brothers are. We both were obsessed with wrestling, formally known as the WWF (World Wrestling Federation). Power slams and clotheslines took up an abundance of our television time. We'd wrestle, he would try moves on me, mostly with my consent. He'd perform "power bombs," which were relatively safe and fun; he'd thrust me up into the air, flip-ping me, and I would land hard on my back, slamming into Dennis and Linda's bed. Once, however, there was no soft landing, he did it on the floor between the bed and the dresser. I didn't rotate the necessary degrees and landed headfirst, the top of my skull smashing into the floor, my neck wrenching. I lay on the floor stiff, I could not move, I could not talk, and I could barely breathe. Staring at the ceiling, Scott panicked above me, kept hushed and whispering, pet-rified he'd get in trouble. He got me to my room and I waited until the pain lessened.

Like any sibling, he could get too rough, whether wrenching my arm until I screamed or putting me in a sleeper hold, making me slip under for a moment, blurred stars dancing in front of a black backdrop. Or hurting me emotionally, throwing my stuffed animals around the room, punching them, beating them, my pleas only hyp-ing him up more. Whether emotional or physical, when it was all too much I would cry, begging him to stop, to leave.

As a kid it was complicated, looking up to him as much as I did, while also experiencing another side, which felt harsh and remorseless. But none of this was Scott's fault, he was a kid, too. Kids can be mean, kids can be rough. It was his mother's encouragement that stung.

"You're such a brat, shut up, you brat," Linda shouted at me from the hall. She looked satisfied, as if having unearthed another perfectly discreet way to induce pain, shrouded in the guise of sibling tension.

Linda's snicker came out when Scott and she would tease me, sometimes evolving into a full cackle. It seemed she'd dig to find anything to pick at, whatever helped her feel better. In retrospect, I think it was compulsive. I am sure Linda didn't *want* to be cruel, but I believe she held an impulse in her depths to habitually come for me.

Private play in my bedroom offered solace. A different bunk bed challenged my architectural capabilities. Sometimes I'd include the desk adjacent to the bed, a tiny nook where one could hide. I adored Playmobil. I craved narrative, drama, relationships, and otherworldly challenges. At my mom's I had a pirate ship and at my father's a Playmobil gas station.

I escaped to my room, eager to go on a journey, an adventure of the imagination, which I found no less thrilling than a "real" adventure, if not more so. I had put on my blue Adidas tracksuit, a prized possession. It was zipped up to the very top that day, ready to go to a space where I could be *exactly* who I was. Nothing between me and the moment, no expectations, no performing, no eviscerating self-doubt. I slipped my arms into the loops of my backpack, which I'd stuffed full of the objects I might require on my adventure—a small wallet with a couple loonies and Canadian Tire money, a plastic sword. I knelt on the bed, making final adjustments to my pack, lost in my imaginary world. I was mentally preparing for my expedition when the door opened and in walked Linda.

She burst into laughter and called for Scott to come see. I heard him scramble out of his room, and he appeared in the doorway next to her. They stood there, looming, just staring in and mocking me, speaking of me as if I was not there. What looked like delight spread across their faces as they teased me. The three of us, alone in the house. Though I'm not sure that my father would have done much had he been there.

He was different when it was just the two of us versus when it was the whole family.

"If Linda and you were drowning, I would save you," he would say in private. "Linda is not the love of my life, you are the love of my life." This was a secret. I knew it was one without him directly saying so, because around Linda the energy was not the same. We had a song, Ruth Brown's "Ain't Nobody's Business." Dennis would blare it, singing along, while driving me to school.

Around Linda that "love" evaporated. A transformation in the tone, the body, the face. A coldness, as if they'd conspired and teamed up, a frigid demeanor that made my eyes fall to the floor. She could be mean to me around the others but was worse to me when we were alone. I've kept these stories close; it's hard even to share fragments of them here. My father did nothing, no protection.

I yearned for time with my father, away from Linda. "You're manipulating your father," she spat once. The words, searing and sharp, they singed, a flash fry leaving a mark. Linda did not like us spending time alone together, every time, without fail, it created friction.

They married when I was ten in our living room in front of the fireplace. I wore a little dress and I sobbed. Linda hugged me as if I was crying tears of joy. As if she loved me. As if we loved each other. I wept more and more. I put on an act, just like I did in all those cards I wrote expressing appreciation and adoration. As if it was a duty. I was an emotional, messy jumble of never wanting to see her again and desperately needing her to love me, the autopilot taking over—stuck on a moving sidewalk.

When I was older and the boys at school were no longer interested in being friends and the girls had distanced themselves or, worse, turned mean, she focused her teasing on my lack of a social life. "Why aren't you more social? Do you just have no friends?" she'd say. There was something in her that liquidated any confidence I had left. My system would malfunction, an invisible force pressing on my limbs. Less a freeze, more a flop.

Scott was assistant captain of his hockey team, which was the best in the league. He was handsome, a ruling jock of the halls. It's difficult to imagine he was not a bully at times, but he did grow up to be a very sensitive man. I have a lot of love for my brother. He bawled his eyes out after the premiere of my film *Freeheld*. Ashley was pretty, smart, and feminine. The ideal popular 1990s girl. Scott and Ashley were social butterflies. Always in and out, always on the phone, making this plan and that plan.

When they were not home I would answer the phone and write down messages for them. *Ashley, Tom called at 4:15 says give him a call back* or *Scott, Kelly called and says she will meet you at Nick's later.* I'd leave the Post-it notes stuck on the side of the island, they'd be waiting for them when they entered the kitchen. Yellow dance cards on display.

Linda's subtext echoed louder than the gulls. Pounding her fists on the evidence, hammering in my loneliness. *Why aren't you like them?*

6

JUMP SCARE

———

The first time the voice said to me *that can't go in your body* I was sixteen, in an Italian restaurant on Queen West in Toronto. A friend, Wiebke, was letting me live with her just around the corner on Claremont Street. She had taken me to dinner to cheer me up after a difficult day.

I met Wiebke not long before I turned fifteen. She'd cast me in her first full-length film, *Marion Bridge*. It premiered at the Toronto International Film Festival in 2002, where Wiebke was awarded Best First Feature. It was a brilliant film that was originally a play by the legendary Cape Bretoner Daniel MacIvor.

Agnes, played by Molly Parker, returns to her hometown to care for her dying mother, having fled a decade earlier to escape a household that was shrouded in vicious abuse. She reunites with her sisters, Theresa and Louise, their wounds half scabbed, the blood seeping out in their own unique ways—that mysterious little goblin named trauma, scuttling through the flesh. I played the object of Agnes's perplexing obsession, a teenager named Joanie working at a gift shop in Marion Bridge, a rural community just twenty minutes from Sydney.

Sitting behind the steering wheel in the gravel parking lot, Agnes sits and stares, eventually mustering up the courage to go inside. Joanie is her biological child, whom she gave away for adoption when she was a teenager. Joanie knows nothing of this. Suspicion grows as Agnes makes recurring visits. Worlds collide, secrets surface, truth laid bare.

The waiter placed our food on the table, snapping me out of a stupor. I stared down at my margherita pizza. Wiebke sat opposite me, lifting the knife provided to cut hers, it had pears and ham. I zoomed out, departing from my body.

Nope. The voice spoke with a sinister tone. *That can't go inside of you.*

I'd had to call the police hours before. I had my first stalker.

It did not begin like that. At first, he became a friend, albeit a secret one. A covert pen pal for the previous two years or so. He had seen me on the CBC family drama *Pit Pony,* which first aired in early February 1999, when I was eleven years old and he was in his early twenties.

Pit Pony was my first professional acting job. My work up until that point was comprised of a couple plays with the drama club in elementary school. For the first role, I was a dove, and I screwed up my one line, leaving a short pause before saying "oops." The audience laughed. The following year, I landed Charlie in *Charlie and the Chocolate Factory* and had a more successful run. The thrill of playing a character so iconic to me, the thrill of playing a boy, organic and free. My bunk bed fort but onstage. Perhaps people would see me?

In 1996, a local actor and casting director named John Dunsworth came to my school. I was nine years old. He was looking to cast the CBC movie of the week, *Pit Pony,* which was based on a young adult book of the same name. I remember him interrupting music class with my favorite teacher, Mr. Ellis, who had once jokingly said I needed to stop "roughing up the boys at recess" to my delight.

We all stood in the class while Mr. Dunsworth had us do little exercises, testing us. I was selected to audition.

I showed up on the day, excited yet not old enough to fully understand the significance. "Could you act like you are lost in the forest?" the casting director prompted. I turned my head swiftly, abruptly from the left to the right, spinning my body around, terrified at the night creeping in, abandoned in the cold dark. A game of imagination.

"That was great. Now could we try it with you being still? Can you show me that feeling with just your emotions?"

I wasn't sure exactly what he meant, but I played along. I must have done something right because I got the part. I couldn't believe it. Another chance to get lost in a pretend world that felt more like reality than my own. It was assumed to be an anomaly, a delightful little surprise. But then the movie of the week turned into a television show, and my acting career began.

I played the little sister, Maggie MacLean. She wore dresses with long sleeves that hung below the knee. Over them, a smock. I was puzzled by the dress over the dress. Black tights covered my legs. My hair had grown out from when we shot the movie of the week, in which I wore a wig. Relentlessly itchy, it resembled a dead raccoon. I didn't want long hair, but I didn't want to wear that wig again. Around my shoulders, sometimes in braids, potentially a small bow. I can only imagine my mother's relief.

Becoming a professional actor coincided with the end of me getting the "thanks, bud" at the mall. Growing my hair out for roles, body on the precipice of change, I would stare at the cis boys on set. Collared shirts, suspenders, knickers, and no tights. Instead of bows, newsboy hats.

How is that not me? I move like them; I play like them.

A gnawing feeling from toddlerhood, stored in the spine, like shingles, striking at a moment's notice, spreading across my body, nerves exposed.

While making *Pit Pony,* my gender dysphoria was rife. The way the tights glued to my body, the way my dresses flowed. Those fucking bows, like the barrettes my mom would snap in my hair, provoking an unresolved, internalized tantrum.

Getting ready for school, solo in the bathroom, I'd smash my head with my hairbrush. *Who is that in the mirror?* Squinting my eyes shut, bracing for it, slam slam slam. My mother's queen bed had a frame that included tall wooden posts on the corners, the tops of them resembling upside-down ice-cream cones. When I was alone, able to keep my secret, I would climb up onto the bed. I'd stare at the post, aligning my torso so the spike would drill directly into my stomach. I'd hoist my body up, conspiring with gravity to impale myself. It hurt but also didn't hurt. I loved having an outlet for my self-disdain, the nausea, I wanted it scooped out.

Sitting in the den at my father's, I'd turn on the family computer, looking for an escape, another pretend world. I had made a silly website in junior high school when we were learning about HTML in computer science class. The man who had seen me on CBC found the website and reached out through it. Over the course of a few emails, a connection began to grow, a companionship. We wrote of our grievances, our loneliness, our incongruence with our surroundings and with ourselves. Kid drama for me, something else for him.

Like one of Pavlov's dogs, my heart palpitated upon hearing that Apple start-up sound. I'd close my eyes, visualizing a new email, jonesing for the serotonin bump. The dial-up internet screeched and scratched and hissed, those irksome noises.

As he started to express deeper feelings for me, my stomach churned. Repressing the gurgles, I stayed on track, I didn't want to lose this, an actual connection with weight, with promise. Even around my friends my panic fluttered. I could not speak to my parents about my emotions, not the true ones at least. Lost in the desert, the barren landscape abundant with life, I just couldn't see it. It felt like he was all I had.

He lived an hour or so outside of Toronto. He wrote that he would be coming to Halifax. The drive from Toronto to Halifax is two days. I had done it many times with my mother to visit my aunts. A small red cooler always sat at my feet on the floor of my mother's red VW Golf, full of snacks and Pepsi, my tiny legs hovered above. I'd crack one open, salivating at that click/ah/hiss. Gulping and digging into a bag of ketchup chips, I would stare out the window and count the passing cows. I especially loved the Guernseys. I could spot them by their tan color, their reddish-brown blotches. I would make my poor mother listen to the *Lion King* soundtrack on loop. How many times she was forced to listen to "Hakuna Matata" I don't know. Me waving my greasy, ketchup chip–stained hands in the air, belting it out. We would spend the night near the Quebec and New Brunswick border. I loved listening to her speak French.

Staring at the glowing computer, I read his words ad nauseam, hoping they would change. My body solid, skin tight, bricks on the chest. I began to perspire, dampness on the neck. Despite sweating, I shook, cold but burning, ears ringing. My first panic attack, in retrospect. I did my best to dodge, intuiting that a clear no would not suffice, that something had changed. Ultimately, I managed to get him not to come and began the process of extracting myself.

Responding less, disappearing for long periods. I could breathe, it seemed like that episode of *Degrassi* had ended.

Not long after I moved to Toronto, he resurfaced, having known my plan to move there in the fall. The emails amped up. He would attach pictures of me with my eyes closed, and photoshop himself with massive angel wings above me, glaring down. They must have been stills he took on his television, they were not images I could remember.

I'm going to cum on you in the clouds of heaven, he wrote.

He'd send me links to missing children websites.

By then I was sixteen years old.

And worst of all, Creed lyrics.

> Above all the others we'll fly
> This brings tears to my eyes
> My sacrifice

He made it increasingly clear that he wasn't going to let anything or anyone get in his way.

Wiebke was the first person I told about him, the emails had reached a sizzling point. The oil leaping from the pan.

"You should really eat, you need to eat," Wiebke said, with a look of concern I appreciated.

That can't go inside of you. That minacious voice again.

"I know, Wiebke, I'm not sure I can."

That can't go inside of you. Insisting.

My stomach felt like a dirty old cloth getting wrung out over the sink, hands choking it, bit by bit.

I tried to eat a bite of the pizza. No matter how much I chomped and gnawed, swallowing was out of the question.

That can't go inside of you. Again, that sardonic inflection.

The flavor had altered, my taste buds spoiled. Leaning over, elbow on table, hand on forehead, I drank some water.

It isn't as if I had *no* food thoughts before. They had started to pop up when puberty launched. I was filling out, growing breasts, all my discomfort heightened as boys and girls disentangled. Watching myself on-screen had not been a problem for me really, but as my body morphed, that changed. The more visible I became, the more I waned.

My pizza still untouched, we headed home. I couldn't shake the events that had happened earlier that day.

"Ellen!" Wiebke yelled.

I was sitting in my room doing homework. I loved that room, it was small, just enough space for a bed and a little dresser. The room had been painted close to canary yellow, my Cat Power and my Peaches posters tacked up. It had one big old window. At night, I would awake to eyes glowing, peering in, the raccoons examining me. There was a whole family in the attic at some point. Over a hundred thousand raccoons live in Toronto, it's been called the Raccoon Capital of the World. The population began to skyrocket when Toronto introduced the "green bin," a municipal compost program, in 2002. Feasts upon feasts.

"Yeah?" I took a right out of my room and entered her office. The original hardwood floors creaked under the feet, the house already eighty years old at that point. She swiveled in her chair to look at me, pale, an email open on the monitor.

Hi, I'm a good friend of Ellen's and I'd really love to surprise her in Toronto. I haven't seen her yet since she moved . . .

A friend then called, telling me she got the same email and thought it suspect. Another pal forwarded his email. He was homing in.

He had virtually all of my contacts. I'd been working since I was ten, having filmed in places as close as Charlottetown, Prince Edward Island, and as far as Saskatoon, Saskatchewan, Berlin, and Lisbon. I could easily imagine a friend in Halifax thinking it was a pal of mine in Ontario. I raced to email everyone I knew, attaching an image of him. He had sent it not long before. A selfie as they are now known, his face filled the screen. Eyes disturbed, he leered at me. Wiebke called the police.

I was relieved when a woman arrived at the door. The officer walked in the house, head rotating, eyes searching every corner, a glance up the stairs. She said hardly anything initially. I imagined her in cop school being taught how to enter a place. The body language, stiff and solid and intentional. The tone flat. The face expressionless. Barely any eye contact at first. She combed the surroundings, assessing the danger. We showed her the emails, the photos, the links, and the lyrics. All of it. She was alarmed. I found myself looking out the window, imagining him suddenly across the street. A quick cut, the jump scare.

They phoned my father to explain the situation. It was a relief to have him know, for my parents to know. I was exhausted from the ceaseless state of disquietude. I took the phone, pressing it to my ear, my heart rate finally beginning to slow. "I'm going to come to Toronto and kick your ass," was the very first thing he said to me.

He was furious. Livid at what I had done, befriending an older man online when I was a kid. I went numb after that, his angry voice fading away, but I will never forget those words. *I'm going to come to Toronto and kick your ass.* All the emails from my stalker paling in comparison.

When the police later went to the stalker's house, he simply asked, "Does this mean I get to see Ellen in court?" Their presence didn't faze him, if anything it titillated him more.

Between that comment, the emails, and his collection of photographs and other material pertaining to me, I was able to get a restraining order.

Every day I'd wait on Ossington Avenue just north of Queen West to catch the 63A to go to school, about a thirty-minute ride. I went to Vaughan Road Academy, where they had a program called Interact. It was one of the main reasons I moved to Toronto.

> If you are involved in dance, theatre, music, or athletics, we offer you our unique integrated program with timetables that are built around your auditions, rehearsals, performances, and competitions . . . This is the only program in Ontario that offers you this type of flexibility. Our focus is to provide you an education that works with your outside interests.

Flashes of him taunted me. Coming up from behind with a knife, stabbing my back. Stepping onto the bus, charging at me, blade penetrating my chest. Waiting when I got off the bus, that last short walk to school, a bullet to the head.

I had to bring his picture to school, handing copies out to my teachers, who presented the photo to the rest of the class in a morbid show-and-tell. I was filming the television show *ReGenesis* at the time, with Mark, who had first told me about Interact. We'd met a year before and become inseparable. When leaving set for the day, the driver would take an obscure route, making sure no one followed. Still, it would be easy to find out where the studio was located. Again, pictures were shown at work. I couldn't stop visualizing him ending my life.

Shortly after, I was walking east down Queen Street West toward Yonge Street where I would catch Line 1 at Queen station, across from the Eaton Centre, Toronto's largest mall. I'd take the nine-stop journey north up to Mark's house, exiting at Eglinton station.

I was on the north side of the street, across from what was the MuchMusic building. For my non-Canadian readers, MuchMusic launched in 1984 and was essentially the Canadian MTV. I felt a hand on my right shoulder, it stroked down to my elbow.

"You look familiar." I turned and saw his face.

He stood in front of me, casual, a hint of a smile. I pictured a knife entering me, shimmering in the sun each time he pulled it out to stab again, a sacrifice. He had made it clear on multiple occasions that no one was going to get in the way of us, our connection, our love. Not my father, not the police.

"Come with me and let's talk."

I noticed a little white dog at his feet. This seemed unusual, he lived almost an hour from the city.

I could not move. I could not speak. *You're going to die now,* I thought. *This is it.*

"Come on, just come with me, we can go talk," he said, trying to persuade me with a gentle tone.

An intoxicating smell of refined sugar wafted out of Cafe Crepe's take-out window, a sweet buckwheat treat. The iconic café with its giant red neon sign was locked in my peripheral vision. Never had I felt that frozen, Encino Man waiting to be found. My chest unlocked. Rise and fall. My lungs returned to their function.

"You can't be here." All I managed to get out, a record skipping. "You can't be here, you can't be here, you can't be here."

People swiped by, flashes behind him, one of the busiest stretches of Toronto. I tried to pull out my focus, dolly back. I raised my voice.

"You can't be here, you can't be standing there!"

Nobody looked.

"Just come with me, we can go for a walk." He took a small step, gesturing toward me.

"Don't hurt me! Don't hurt me!" I shouted, bidding on *don't hurt me* to attract pedestrians' attention. Stepping back, I put my hands up. "Don't hurt me, don't hurt me!"

Passersby craned their necks. No one interfered but it was sufficient, causing him to retreat. He took off, the little dog marching at his feet.

I fled. Running, I wove in and out, zigzagging through streets. In retrospect a fruitless endeavor, assuming he had discovered my address. I called my father the moment I got home. At first he didn't believe me.

The police were notified. The man was arrested, having not complied with the restraining order. I didn't press charges.

It turned out he had undiagnosed schizophrenia. We came to a settlement of sorts. He would live with his father and begin mental health treatment. He would not come near me or contact me in any shape or form, which he has not. It all ended rather abruptly. And if there is a tiny morsel of goodness in all of this, it's that he was finally seen. He could now receive support for his pain. Perhaps that was all he was asking for? I hope he got the help he needed, I hope he never did this again.

I managed to forgive him, but it wasn't easy. There was a lot at play when I would abuse my body, having done it since I was a small child. This event hurled it all forward. As if I was running through an unconscious checklist:

1. People cut themselves, I'll try that.
2. People get wasted, I'll try that.
3. People stop eating, I'll try that.
4. People repress, I'll try that.

I would take a small knife to my room, place the tip on my upper arm, close to the shoulder. Pressing down, dragging it slightly, enough to see that red, enough for that relief. That did not last long. I got wasted one night by myself in Toronto, *this is something people do to help,* my brain divulged. I drank vodka straight from a juice glass at the small blue chrome dining table in the kitchen. Sipping, then tipping the bottle for more. Poor Wiebke came home to a wasted, emo teenager, Broken Social Scene's "Anthems for a Seventeen-Year-Old Girl" on repeat.

> Used to be one of the wretched ones and I liked you
>   for that
> Now you're all gone, got your makeup on and you're
>   not coming back
> Can't you come back?

Number three is what stuck. It seemed to be the solution, food restriction my new norm. This all coincided with puberty, my body continuing to develop, but not like Mark's. Reality settled in, I would never see myself in the mirror, I'd forever feel this disgust, and I punished my body for it. Research has shown that transgender and gender-nonconforming youth are four times more likely to struggle with an eating disorder.

My brain became consumed by counting calories, time passing, how to make myself full without making myself full. When to make the clear herbal tea that satiated my gut just enough. Endless gum chewing. Avoiding. I'd measure my All-Bran in the morning, the soy milk, too. Dismissing Wiebke's concerns, I'd bring a protein bar to school for lunch and allow myself to eat only half of it. At least the flashes of him had dissipated. At least walking down the street I could stress about bread instead of the residual terror. A knife in the back. Putting my fear in a sandwich so I could control it. So I could forget it.

It is not as easy to forgive my father. *I'm going to come to Toronto and kick your ass.* When his kid needed safety, when his kid needed love, when his kid needed protection, he threatened violence. Outraged because I had the audacity to communicate with an older man on the internet when I was a minor. If I didn't deserve care in that moment, if I didn't deserve safety and love, when would I ever? That sentence has lived in my body much longer than the man's threats, his obsession, his fingers fondling my arm.

7

LEECHES

———

I learned early on I could not have my parents at work with me. Sitting on a small wooden swing, I was filming a scene of *Pit Pony* in the front yard of the MacLean family home in Cape Breton. I was acting with Shaun Smyth, an astute actor, understated and nuanced. We swayed gently as his character consoled mine, his hands dirty from coal. I liked him; he was handsome, slightly gruff but kind. Working with kids can be a lot, and I appreciated his generosity and patience.

My father was in my periphery. My focus went from the moment in the scene to my dad with his 1970s Nikon taking black-and-white photographs. I clamped shut, that freezing again. Whatever that thing was I could supposedly do—create an honest emotion with an expressiveness that the adults said translated to the screen— abruptly stopped when I felt his presence.

A similar sensation occurred when my mom would watch. This was around when I was arriving at the age where being a tomboy was no longer a cute look. The lurking pressure to change was omnipresent, a consistent state of disapproval. I imagine she may have prayed for me to not be gay. I needed some space.

At eleven, I had asked them to hide if I was shooting, but that wasn't enough. No longer could I release myself to the emotion, that sensation, the rush that I loved, it would stop. Eventually I suggested they not come at all. They did not take it personally, even though I was unable to articulate the why of it all. It shocked me that I had asked for what I needed, despite being afraid, and that someone had listened. Perhaps they were relieved. They both worked full-time and often it wasn't even possible for them to show up.

For the second season of *Pit Pony,* the horse wranglers, Lee and Jerry, and their sixteen-year-old daughter, Fallon, were my chaperones. They were kind and let me live with them. They had a house that was close to the soundstage and a ranch about a twenty-minute drive from Sydney in Leitches Creek. We would swim in the river on their property, and I would practice flipping my wet hair to the right like the other boys did when they emerged from the water. We would pick leeches from our bodies, just grabbing and yanking, unbothered. It made me feel like the young guys in *Stand by Me,* except they were terrified of the leeches and I was not. It made me feel brave. Did that up my chances to achieve my dream, to look like River Phoenix in a white T-shirt?

Despite playing and having to dress like a girl in 1904 while working, these times let me be closer to the boy I was. I was somewhere new, with adults, people who had not known me before. I was making friends, real ones, the kind who encouraged my feelings, championing that little guy, letting him breathe. I had an opportunity to exist as myself, start from scratch, the cool loner on the ranch. This freedom on and off set transferred to the work. I loosened up. I was happy.

My parents almost never came to work with me ever again. If

they did, it was just a visit, but I would not allow them to come to set. This increased my vulnerability in ways, I'm sure, but having witnessed some of the worst stage parents you could imagine, I am glad I experienced the other version. I've watched adults slowly chip away at their children, their overprotection a form of neglect. If they were a character in a screenplay the first note would be "too much," but they aren't *actually* watching, they aren't *really* listening. All the value wrapped up in work, in image, in followers. The opposite of what acting should be, a disintegration of ego, not the stroking of one. It ends careers.

Even though I preferred my path, my lack of healthy boundaries still did not bode well. As puberty transmuted me into a character I had no interest in playing, my isolation, insecurity, and unknowing grew. I desperately needed to anchor myself. In new cities, with no friends, alone in hotel rooms, it was not hard for someone to prey. I'm sure they sense that. Like the man I met online. A lonely kid is a perfect target.

There was the director who groomed me when I was a teenager. His frequent texts made me feel special, as did the books he gifted me. He took me to dinner at Swan on Queen West. Stroking my thigh under the table, he whispered: "You have to make the move, I can't."

On a project not long before, a crew member had done the same. In between takes he would talk to me about art and films, Kubrick naturally. He invited me to hang out on a Saturday afternoon. After a walk in the rain he grabbed me, asserting we go upstairs. Pulling me in to his body, I could feel his hard cock against me.

Just before I turned eighteen, I filmed my first movie in Los Angeles. I hadn't made a film in America before, and it was the first time I'd been to LA. I stayed at the Oakwood Apartments in

Burbank, tucked into a hill right off Barham Boulevard. Famous for all the child stars who have passed through, Neil Patrick Harris, Kirsten Dunst, Jennifer Love Hewitt. The property was always teeming with stage parents.

Hard Candy begins with a successful photographer named Jeff, played by the illustrious Patrick Wilson, chatting with a fourteen-year-old girl online. The plot hard to believe considering what had just transpired with my stalker. The banter is flirty, youthful. They meet up, he takes her home in his Mini, we are concerned for Hayley. They are drinking. Jeff wants to take photos, his tone shifts to frustration, aggression peeking through. However, the tables turn. A spiked screwdriver brings him to the floor and he wakes up tied to a chair.

Hayley believes he is involved in the kidnapping and murder of a girl her age, and makes it clear to him that if he doesn't confess, she will castrate him, a shockingly simple surgery that she has taught herself to do as an honors student. She freezes his dick with a giant bag of ice. Jeff is in agony, hands turning blue, pleading desperately, swearing he had no involvement. He screams, but it's useless. Hayley performs the procedure and dumps his testicles down the kitchen sink. Jeff can hear the garbage disposal masticating his balls.

Ultimately, she doesn't really perform the surgery, but Jeff does admit to being involved. "I just took pictures," he says. *Just* a pedophile.

We shot the film, almost all of it, in a small studio close by the Oakwood Apartments. Burbank, often considered the media capital of the world, is home to Walt Disney Studios, Warner Bros., Nickelodeon Animation Studio, and a massive porn industry. The majority of *Hard Candy* was filmed on a set. The interior of Jeff's house was sleek, minimal, that mid-century cool. The ever-hip professional, Mini-driving, sensitive guy. The friend who could never.

There was a man working on the film who always carried a small book of crosswords, the most formidable ones, I was told. He has since gone on to make films of his own. He was funny and strange, and he was kind to me. We spoke about books, discussed films and obscure, depressing graphic novels. A glint in his eyes made me feel seen, supported. He had a sweetness even.

We made the film in eighteen and a half days, an all-consuming, emotional sprint. I was giddy with exhaustion by the end. The *Hard Candy* wrap party was held in downtown Los Angeles, an elevator ride up a tall building. There was a rare camaraderie among all of us, what you hope for when creating something. We drank and danced and had tearful goodbyes.

My crossword puzzle friend gave me a ride back to the Oakwood Apartments. We drove through the cluster of downtown skyscrapers that towered over us ominously. It was very late, and I laid my head against the window as we got on the 101. I loved the glow of the freeways at night.

Pulling up to the Oakwood, I watched him type in the security code and the gate opened slowly. He walked me to the apartment, followed me in. He stood noticeably close, his body brushing my behind. His voice sweet, his hands on my shoulders, he guided me to the bedroom. I went stiff with a smile. Unsure what to do as he stood tall and removed his glasses. He laid me down on the bed. Starting to remove my pants, he said, "I want to eat you out." I froze. After it was over, he tried to stay in the bed with me. I had thawed marginally and told him he couldn't, to get out. He slept on the couch.

Turning eighteen further frayed my boundaries, an unspoken permission slip I didn't consent to. At the start of a project, a crew member offered to take me apartment hunting on the weekend. It was a nice gesture, but something felt odd. It was far beyond a typi-cal action for someone in her job position. I'd been staying in a hotel up until that point and needed out, a proper fridge at least, so I said yes. She picked me up in her black Audi.

We arrived at the first building, a new development. We met someone in the lobby who took us in the elevator to the top floor. She asked for the person to let us go in on our own to look around the barely furnished apartment. They waited in the hall as we went in. It was a two-bedroom, which was unnecessary, accentuating my loneliness. The apartment was eerily sparse and echoey as we walked through. There wasn't a whole lot to look at, making it feel even more pointless.

I was standing in the empty living room, in front of the couch, when I felt her grab me. She pressed her face into mine, some ver-sion of kissing. That freezing coming over me again. The next thing I knew I was on the rug, the floor firm on my back. I didn't say no, I did not resist, I just stiffened. Lying on the carpet, I didn't make a sound. She began to dry hump me, at first slow, then faster and faster, her body on top of me, the weight grinding my spine into the floor. Her eyes were closed, head turned away from me, face per-spiring. She huffed and puffed and began to moan. I didn't move, just stared up at the ceiling, then closed my eyes, then looked up again as she came. It was only the second time I had kissed a woman and the first time I had ever seen one come in person.

This dynamic continued. She'd pick me up at my apartment, take me to hers, where a version of the same situation would play out. Me in bed, motionless, frozen, she on top of me, touching me, going inside of me. My rigidness would upset her, my numbness taking over, unable to touch her. We'd get back in the Audi and she'd drop me off at the sterile, one-bedroom apartment I ended up renting. She'd fuck me at work in my trailer. I'd sit on her lap and not know why.

I was back in the same city two years later to make another film. Memories of her still lingered, the heavy breathing and the sweating above me. The arching of her back when she came. More than half-way into the shoot I arrived at work at the crack of dawn. As I was walking to my trailer I noticed a black Audi and my heart stopped. *It can't be,* I thought. But I knew it was.

"Darren is out for the day so someone else is filling in," another person on set mentioned.

I ducked into my trailer and tried to calm my breathing. There was a knock on my door. I opened it and there she was. Standing there, looking up and smiling.

"Hi! Can I come in?" she asked.

I let her in.

"It's nice to see you! We had fun, right?"

What? I thought, nothing actually coming out.

"We had fun, right? We just like, listened to music and had fun, right?"

Her eyes were wide. Her smile almost concealed it, but I could see the fright seeping through.

"Yeah," I responded.

8

FAMOUS ASSHOLE AT PARTY

———

I stayed at a friend's place in the Hills for a few weeks when I was twenty-seven. Someone had been visiting my house in the night, laying roses along the gate. They were leaving notes with quotes from some of my favorite writers and musicians but offered no indication of their own identity. Cryptic messages with unknown intent, something I was familiar with. I decided to leave my house briefly while I had security cameras installed. The home was situated at the very top of the hill, overlooking the city. At night, a sea of lights sprawled below me. I could sit there for hours, transfixed. The glinting and dancing, the red lights a blood current in the veins of LA.

I had not left the house much. My friend was away working, and I was still mending from a heartbreak. I had to force myself to do something. I drove a short distance west to celebrate a good pal's birthday. I arrived at the house party, taking in the unique layout. The extremely high ceilings felt church-like, with a loft where the kitchen and dining area looked down at the vast living room. It was old, perhaps built in the 1940s, a dollhouse occupied by a very hip person. Off the living room, there was a large wooden terrace with built-in benches that overlooked a family of trees and a neighbor's home. This particular friend is a social butterfly, adored by many, so the party was popping, surging with energy. People milked it for every last drop before the inevitable arrival of the cops demanding quiet.

It was 2014, and I had come out as gay only two months before at a Human Rights Campaign conference in Vegas called Time to Thrive, the inaugural event focusing on LGBTQ+ youth. I flew the morning of Valentine's Day to Vegas with my manager. Boarding the flight at Burbank Airport, my anxiety was at a different level. I barely spoke, staring ahead at nothing. On the flight, I obsessively read the speech, as if I could exhaust the emotion, mutating it into that old take-out menu in your kitchen drawer you glance at arbitrarily for no reason. When we arrived at the hotel, all I could do was cradle myself in the hotel bed. No television, no looking at my phone, I just wrapped my arms around my body, time like sludge, barely budging.

As I waited backstage I squeezed my hands together, eyes down, desperate to not have a panic attack. *What if I just collapse onstage?*

I didn't collapse. I managed to make it through the speech without being overcome by emotion, by the catharsis. I floated after, a lightness, a shock to the system. *I did it.* It wasn't until I got in the car to head to the airport that I completely broke down. Sobs of relief. Letting it out.

A weight lifted from my shoulders that I once believed would live there forever. One of the most important and healing moments in my life, not all the way there yet, but getting closer.

My friend's birthday party was in full swing, and I tried to channel the same lightness I'd felt only a few weeks back. I sat outside on one of the benches on the patio, nursing a tequila soda. I caught up with friends and acquaintances I had not seen in ages, even met some new people. I was enjoying myself. An acquaintance of mine arrived, already quite inebriated. He walked out onto the terrace. I said hello. We sometimes saw each other at the gym. His energy was different tonight, harsh. He began by insulting my personality, which okay go for it, but then it moved into another territory.

"I see what you are doing. I'm not stupid. I see what you are doing." He stood too close. Staring down at me where I sat.

"What am I doing?" I answered flatly. More confused than anything. At his aggression, his malevolent smile.

"Oh please. It's obvious what you're doing. The attention."

I was familiar with this tone, this body language—threatening but casual. Flaunting his power. But it took me a moment to process what he might be alluding to.

"Is this about me being gay?"

Spurred, somehow provoked, he sat on the bench next to me and started to lay in.

"That doesn't exist. You aren't gay. You are just afraid of men." He said it ruthlessly, loud but with a smile. Gloating. Responding was useless. It was making it worse. He just kept going. People were telling him to stop, but he didn't, and they gave up.

I stood up and crossed to the other side of the terrace, trying to remove myself from the situation. He followed, sitting next to me again, his body close.

"You're just afraid of men. Men are predators and you're just afraid of them."

He spoke to me as if no opinion mattered but his own. A stroke of wisdom to bestow upon me. Wasted slurs of words vomited out of his body as my body compacted, elbows on alert.

I told him to stop harassing me, to fuck off, that he was being extremely offensive. I got up again and went inside. He pursued behind. I sat down on a small sofa, and he did, too. People danced to the *Spring Breakers* soundtrack, breaking it down to "Scary Monsters and Nice Sprites."

> Look at this
> I'm a coward, too
> You don't need to hide, my friend
> For I'm just like you

"I'm going to fuck you to make you realize you aren't gay. I'm going to lick your asshole. It is going to taste like lime. You're not gay," he slurred. He kept describing how he was going to fuck me, touch me, lick me. How he liked to pity fuck women.

I don't know why I didn't demand he leave, ask for people to do more than "Yo, leave her alone." Some of my closest friends were there, witnessing it. Power works in funny ways. He was, and still is, one of the most famous actors in the world.

I got up and walked to the bathroom. Nervous he was following me, I closed the door and locked it. I sat down on the toilet and looked out the window at the trees, the light from the terrace just barely reaching them. I wondered if anyone could see in, which reinforced a certain aloneness. I stayed on the toilet longer than I needed to, washed my hands, and then left the party.

The incident went on for so long and so many people saw and heard that the following day a friend of mine who wasn't at the party got a text from another friend who wasn't at the party saying, "I heard [he] was horrible to Ellen last night."

A few days later, I was upstairs at the gym, on the treadmill. I was watching the news as I ran by myself when I heard his voice. I'm not sure how he knew I was upstairs but he came bounding up.

"People are saying I need to apologize to you, but I don't remember anything. I'm not like that at all, I'm not prejudiced. I don't know why that happened. I'm sorry. I'm sorry I don't remember anything."

I didn't stop running. Or slow down.

"You clearly have a problem with gay people, you were saying horrific things to me. And not that I care about the consequences you would face, but you're just lucky no one filmed that," I responded.

"I really don't have a problem with gay people, I swear."

My feet pounded.

"I think you might."

He stood there, stunned. He said sorry again and again. I've seen him a couple times since. He barely says hi and neither do I.

I sensed spite from some people in the industry, a hostility even. That flash of aggression, hidden in "jokes," blamed on alcohol, the sexual harassment dismissed.

I remember sitting in a former agent's office, thrilled that VICE wanted to make *Gaycation*. We'd be in Japan in just a couple months to film the first episode. When one of the major players of the agency walked in, I shared the news.

"We get it, you're gay!" he responded instantly.

It's as if there is a need to trivialize such endeavors, unwilling to acknowledge experiences that are not their own, unwilling to listen. Throwing around power but refusing to admit they have any. I wasn't able to stand up for myself then. I'd fold in, taking it, letting it rest inside.

I was persuaded to reject a character not long before I came out as gay because it "wouldn't be helpful." Subtext: people think you're a homo and this will make them think you are definitely a homo and you can't exist as who you are if you want to have a career. The same ongoing conversation, just a new situation for it. I got off that phone call with my agent and started to cry. The bucket full, on the verge of rushing out. I called my manager. I told her I couldn't do it anymore, that I couldn't hide, lie, it was eating me from the inside out.

I said onstage in Vegas:

> Beyond putting yourself in one box or another, you worry about the future. About college or work or even your physical safety. Trying to create that mental picture of your life—of what on earth is going to happen to you—can crush you a little bit every day. It is toxic and painful and deeply unfair.
>
> If we took just five minutes to recognize each other's beauty, instead of attacking each other for our differences. That's not hard. It's really an easier and better way to live. And ultimately, it saves lives. Then again, it's not easy at all. It can be the hardest thing, because loving other people starts with loving ourselves and accepting ourselves.

Coming out in 2014 was more a necessity than a decision, but yes, it was one of the most crucial things I have ever done for myself. No matter what came after, a different kind of exposure, vulnerability, it was all worth it. All a step. I'd rather feel pain while living than hiding. My shoulders opened, my heart was bare, I could be in the world in ways that felt impossible before—*holding hands*. But deep down an emptiness lurked. That undertone. Its whisper still ripe and in my ear.

9

PINK DOT

——

It's 2022, springtime. I had just had dinner with a friend and was headed back to my hotel in West Hollywood. Walking back, heading east along Sunset Boulevard, I texted Madisyn. A mutual friend had set us up about a month before. She was, is, smart, compassionate, fun, and our sex was unbridled yet safe. Perhaps the most uninhibited sex I've had, this new body offering a grounding, a presence. Enjoying things I never thought I would. Feeling queerer than ever. How deeply freeing to have someone love fucking my dick and my pussy and permitting myself to enjoy it. No longer frozen, that undercurrent, the wanting to flee.

When Madisyn arrived we immediately started to kiss, a physical chemistry that takes control, magnets sucking. I moved down her body to my knees, her hand resting on my head, ever so slightly pulling my hair. We had sex for hours and then slept deeply. I almost always wake up around six, and I snuck out of the room, trying not to wake her. I drank coffee and sat at my computer to write. I love the early morning, the quiet, a certain kind of healthy loneliness. A reminder?

The hotel was on Sunset Boulevard. I planned to stay for six days to see friends I'd missed dearly during the height of the pandemic. Every hello and goodbye hit in a new way now. I'd flown in from New York City, having moved three years ago from LA, where I'd been for the previous ten years. I lived various places, Hancock Park, Beachwood Canyon, Studio City, and lastly in Nichols Canyon, not far from where I was staying. West Hollywood is known as an LGBTQ+ area of Los Angeles. Rows of queer bars run along Santa Monica Boulevard, mostly catering to cis white gay men. Rainbows line the streets.

I wrote all morning. Madisyn joined me at the table at nine thirty, her sweatpants and vintage T-shirt made me hard, I have a thing for sweatpants. We both sat and did work. We spent time together well. There was a natural flow, lucid, not forced, and fine with silence.

We wrote then fucked then ate then napped and then I left the hotel for the first time at around four to go to Pink Dot, a convenience store directly across the street on Sunset. Known for its colorful pink and light blue exterior, and the vintage blue VW Bug with pink dots and a propeller hat parked out front.

While walking the short distance from the hotel exit to the southeast corner of Sunset and La Cienega, I passed a tall man who I briefly caught eyes with. He carried a slushy in one hand and a plastic bag in the other. As I neared the corner, the light red, cars hurtling down Sunset, he turned and started to move toward me.

"Don't look at me, you fucking faggot! Faggot!" He screamed this at me, over and over. Every *faggot* getting louder. No one near us on the sidewalk.

He was about three feet away, standing over me. I froze. There was no room for me to tell him I was, in fact, not looking at him. He just kept yelling. I worried that if I turned to run it could trigger a reaction, and the same if I said something. So I just stood solid, looking forward, doing my best to seem unaffected. And in the moment I was, because I was in shock. This seemed to work, he started to walk east a bit. I took out my phone and called Madisyn. Better not to text, you can keep your head up if you're on the phone. Shaken, I explained and asked if she could come over to Pink Dot. The call triggered him. As the light finally changed and I stepped off the curb, he turned back around.

"Don't you fucking talk about me, faggot. I know you're talking about me. I'm going to beat you up, fag!"

He charged toward me from behind, yelling at me, Madisyn hearing all this through the phone.

"I'm going to fucking gay bash you, faggot."

He started coming faster. This time I ran, trying to reach Pink Dot before he reached me. That jolt of panic, a flashback to being with Justin on the hill or when another man in West Hollywood, years before, screamed, "I'm going to beat you into the ground, you ugly fucking dyke. I'll kill you before the police get here." My friend Angela and I sped away in her car. Or when I ran from a group of teenage girls who surrounded me at eighteen. "It isn't Halloween. Why are you dressed up as a lesbian?" one of them asked as they approached, threatening me. Or when Paula and I dodged a friend of a friend who came at us around a bonfire, wasted and enraged by our snuggling. "You don't have to shove it in our faces!" he barked. Others had to intervene, fighting him off until he stumbled away.

"This is why I need a gun!" the man yelled right behind me as I frantically swung open the door to Pink Dot.

"Please help! This guy is screaming at me, calling me a faggot and saying he is going to bash me." The words flew out of my mouth. As I swung my head over my shoulder and back.

I was out of breath, my voice trembled, but I tried to suppress it. The man stood right outside the entrance. Two people were working behind the desk. One of them jetted toward the door, yelling at the man to get away, locking it as the pursuer lingered, but then walked off. The woman at the counter asked if I needed water, she encouraged me to breathe.

"We don't put up with that here," she said. "Are you okay? You sure I can't get you anything?"

I said I was fine but thanked them, taking her advice to breathe, to calm my nerves.

I have learned to compartmentalize these moments for the most part. Shut down. Shrug my shoulders. Let it run off my back like the beer I had thrown on me while walking down Queen West in Toronto less than six months before while filming the third season of *The Umbrella Academy*. Another queer-friendly neighborhood. My friend Genesis and I passed a man who proceeded to turn around and throw his beer at the backs of our heads.

"Faggots! Faggots!" he said as he walked away. The *s* slithered, *ssss,* like poison down the throat. That time, I pivoted, a reflex, boiling rage from all the times I hadn't turned around.

"Did you just call me a fucking faggot? Fuck you!" I yelled, repeatedly, as a few people standing on the sidewalk watched. Genesis pleaded for me to calm down. He walked off.

I think about that moment a lot—the anger that man felt entitled to display and my response to it. In our society anger and masculinity are so intertwined—I hope to redefine that in my own life.

I forgot I had hung up on Madisyn when I frantically swung open the door to Pink Dot. I could see her on the other side of the street, already on the way over. The man was nowhere in sight, so I expressed my gratitude for the help and walked to the sidewalk to meet her, my neck twisting from side to side. I made sure to keep looking as we walked the short distance back to the hotel room.

She put her arm around me as I recounted what had happened, the touch different from before.

10

THAT LITTLE INDIE

———

I didn't get my first tattoo until I was thirty, but the meaning stretched back to one of my earlier experiences as an actor. The tattoo reads c keens, and it's located on my upper right arm, just below the shoulder. c keens is my nickname for one of my dearest friends, Catherine Keener. I met her during a pivotal time, post–*Hard Candy,* pre-*Juno,* I was busy but not very known. Groundless in Los Angeles, sprawled and unfamiliar. I was researching for my next role, up all night digesting the horrors, hoping my acting partner and I would get along, that we would trust each other. I was finding it hard to separate myself from my roles, and this role was particularly distressing.

My initial meeting with Catherine was at her home in Santa Monica, just a few minutes' walk from the beach. At nineteen, I had just signed on to star in *An American Crime* with her. Tommy O'Haver, the writer and director, picked me up from a hotel in Hollywood on Highland Boulevard. We drove the forty minutes west to her home so Catherine and I could spend time there together. Talk the film, the characters, but mostly connect with each other. These weren't easy roles.

The house was an old dark-brown Craftsman. It had an unusually large backyard, the kind you do not expect in Santa Monica. A small tree house, a swing dangling below. Tall hedges stretched above the surrounding fence. It felt like its own little world.

The fact that I had been cast opposite such an icon was utterly surreal for me. I'd be making a film with one of my favorite actors of all time. Stepping through her back gate, I was unbearably shy. I barely spoke.

I had attempted to look cool. Vintage T, black jacket, torn-up Converse. She walked toward us with a giant smile and that familiar voice. Wearing ripped jeans and a baggy white T-shirt, she oozed warmth and sincerity. She was direct, with characteristic sensual swagger.

We climbed over her deck balcony and continued our way up to the roof. Our sense of humor aligned, and her unmistakable laugh came pouring out. Staring out toward the Pacific, we spoke of what was ahead. No condescension, that dismissive cadence slung at you when you're young. Instead an unspoken ease. I'd never met anyone like her before.

I went from shy to present. I could already feel her care, her desire to protect, but with zero preciousness. We became pals quickly, but our closeness could only do so much to mitigate the effect filming had on my nineteen-year-old self.

An American Crime was based on a true story about a sixteen-year-old girl, Sylvia Likens, who in 1965 suffered the most amount of abuse on a single victim in Indiana state history. The film is brutal, but it holds back, the real story was even worse. I had been cast as Sylvia.

Sylvia's parents were carnival workers, and when they traveled, they left two of their daughters with Gertrude Baniszewski. Keener played Gertrude, a single mother of seven, struggling with poverty, barely earning a living by doing laundry for her Indianapolis neighbors. Gertrude almost never ate, her face gaunt, angular, and sharp, a body as thin as a rake. She self-medicated with downers, swigs from tiny bottles, mood swings fluctuated from one extreme to the other. Sylvia's parents leave Sylvia and their younger daughter, Jennie, with Gertrude and her swaths of kids for twenty dollars a week.

When the first of the money is late, Gertrude takes it out on Sylvia and Jennie. Leading them down to the basement, she demands they bend over and aggressively flogs them. The abuse escalates, Gertrude encouraging her children to join in as well. In one of the most horrifying scenes to film, Gertrude forces Sylvia to stick a Coke bottle up her vagina in front of the other children.

We did not actually do this in front of the younger actors. They only came to set for their coverage. Off camera we pretended Gertrude only twisted Sylvia's arm.

The Coke bottle scene culminates in her being dragged toward the basement steps. Screaming and crying, she is hurled down the stairs. Smashing her head on the cement floor, Sylvia is left with serious blunt force trauma.

There were scenes in my previous films that had been difficult to shoot—violent, sexual, and physical. But this was different. Moments in this film were unspeakably brutal. As a teenager, I did not have the skills to turn it on and off as abruptly and easily as I can now. To leave the work at work. The scenes would linger, feelings stuck. It took longer to dislodge from the body.

During Sylvia's last moment alive, she was branded. Gertrude straddled her while one of the kids held Sylvia's hands above her head. Someone passed out in the theater during this scene when the film premiered at Sundance in 2007. I don't blame them. Sylvia died not long after that. Torment written in her flesh.

Sylvia's body faded away until it broke. Knowing that the story was true made it all worse, the details even more gut churning. I couldn't escape Sylvia, and the days came home with me.

If I was alone in my apartment, I would pace. Walk then sit. Up again, pace. Look out the window, pivot to the bathroom. Windowsill again, sit and smoke. Cigarette done. Grab the backpack and get out. My incessant, underlying need to flee, my new normal. Stopping is too risky, that's when the feelings jump out. Playing a character that was partially starved to death allowed me to lean in to my desire to disappear, to punish myself.

"It's for a film," I'd say in response to a mention of my small bites, the annoying, concerned tone, almost a challenge.

I'll prove to you all that I need nothing. The little voice would brag with the creak of a side smile.

In agony, Sylvia would scratch the concrete floor until the tips of her fingers wore off, she chewed her lip compulsively, biting through the pain. When they found her body it looked as though she had two mouths.

I'm hungry.

Two more hours, then you can eat.

What am I going to eat?

Steamed vegetables and brown rice . . . half of it.

How much more time?

One hour and forty-five minutes.

I'd shower at night, washing off the burns, the bruises, a reminder that I had nothing to complain about. *How dare I acknowledge my silly pain as anywhere near hers.*

I listened to "Downtown" by Petula Clark incessantly. It was one of the most popular songs in 1965, the year Sylvia was murdered.

And you may find somebody kind to help and
　　understand you
Someone who is just like you and needs a gentle hand

Walking, I would listen. On the bus down Sunset, I would listen. In the house, sitting on the windowsill smoking a cigarette, I would listen. It was compulsive, a way I tend to be with songs, some for stranger reasons than others.

I would walk down the hill to Sunset Boulevard, catching the bus west to Hollywood. I'd get off around Vine and wander into Amoeba Music, a warehouse-size new-and-used record, CD, and DVD store in Los Angeles. The tack tack tack of potential buyers flipping through the hard plastic cases filled the ears as much as the latest, hippest songs they played, a metronome setting the speed. It helped the time pass.

Characters affected me in various ways, how could they not? It's an exploration of another human's experience. A never-ending exercise in empathy, opening the heart, hoping it all sinks in, waiting for that release of emotion. My eyes would close, and it would strike me, an inconceivable depth of despair. I wondered how she even made it as long as she did. How she didn't just give up. I guess that is what torture is, dragging you to the end and pulling you back, again and again.

I was staying in Silver Lake in the top floor of a two-story house that had been converted into its own apartment. A one-bedroom with large windows that offered a beautiful view of the city. It was tucked into the hill on Lucile, not far from Sunset Boulevard, but isolated, a substantial, steep climb. I was alone; I had next to no friends in Los Angeles at the time.

I remember Keener scooping me up in her black sedan and taking me to a July Fourth BBQ in the backyard of a house formerly owned by Buster Keaton. I think she wanted to help me, sensing a struggle I could not speak to. We sat down across from her friend Karen O, who I idolized. *Show Your Bones,* a quintessential record for me at the time. But food was stressful, drinking was stressful, my eyeballs darted around, calculations in my brain that refused me the moment.

I was lightly seeing a guy at the time. We would go to dinner and I would just stare at the menu, dazed. I wanted none of it. We sat in a restaurant in a train car that served only pasta. Without ordering, we left, and he drove me home.

"I've already dealt with my issues," he said before pulling away.

"I think I'm gay," I said once while we were fucking. Closed off, disassociated, not even performative.

"No you're not," he responded, continuing with the pumps.

I was barely eating, barely sleeping, delirious on set. I smoked compulsively. Hoping to blow out all the thoughts. Or as Kurt Vonnegut puts it, "The public health authorities never mention the main reason many Americans have for smoking heavily, which is that smoking is a fairly sure, fairly honorable form of suicide."

The shoot became increasingly difficult. I'd crash at Keener's sometimes, especially after the more horrifying days. I felt taken care of there. We'd drink tequila and sit around her firepit. We would blare music and dance dance dance, a wide expanse of unknown adventures ahead. We met making a film wherein she murders me. In the real world she was the only thing saving me.

By the end of the shoot, I had lost a significant amount of weight. And it continued to plummet when I returned to Halifax, where I was still living on and off. I dropped to eighty-four pounds. My arms were so skinny I could take the outer sleeve of a to-go coffee cup, stick my hand through and slide it up my arm, beyond my elbow and to my shoulder. Wasting away. Later that year, I dressed up as a coffee cup sleeve for Halloween—WARNING HOT BEVERAGE INSIDE—spelled out with a thick black marker.

No matter the words or looks of concern or how many rich pastries people tried to get me to eat, I could not see it. I refused to. Hurting my body to that extreme must have been a cry for help, but when the help would come, it made me angry and resentful. *Where have you been?* An unfair question really. I had never communicated what I'd been grappling with to anyone.

When I first returned home my mother's face was filled with panic. The worry in her eyes shattered me, a look of anguish I had not seen before, and the culprit was me. I had crossed a threshold, my weight so low the emaciation had become visible. The sunken cheeks scared me.

My need to fix her, to protect her, forced my eating issue in an alternate direction. Now I *did* want to eat, I was desperate to. I didn't want her to feel that way.

Finally motivated to eat, I couldn't. I'd prepare to take a bite of a sandwich, something simple, nothing fancy. My throat would clench, the back of my neck would grow moist, my chest swelling with deep dread. Spinning into a full panic attack, I could not swallow the food. Having been obsessed with maintaining control, I'd now lost it. Squeezed far too tight. My body, understandably, was done with me.

That will not go in. That will not go in. That will not go in.

My days revolved around the moments I was supposed to get food down. There was no hiding it now, my face cadaverous, body skin and bones. I could not escape the stress, the concern omnipresent.

And I could not shake Sylvia. I thought of her all the time. No role had stuck with me like that. Flashes of the basement. The hunger. Forced to eat her own vomit. Screams ignored.

"How about you try putting cheese sauce on your broccoli?" a well-meaning therapist suggested.

I sat in her office near the Dalhousie University campus, a white room, credentials framed, she had long, wavy, light hair and wore glasses. She had a smile that was stuck on her face.

"Nuts are a great snack to have around."

The conversation revolved around when and what I should eat for breakfast, when and what I should eat for a snack, outlines of what should be on my supper plate. I wasn't supposed to exercise, no push-ups or anything of the sort. Nothing beyond food. And it was all beyond food.

I avoided the few friends I had in Halifax. I was ashamed. The "actress" goes off and returns like all the others. I was such a goddamn cliché. Social anxiety was already a prevalent aspect of my life and as my mental health suffered, my isolation intensified, just a text to a friend seemed out of reach. The idea of making a plan unfeasible.

Loneliness had always been a staple for me, an inherent disconnect from my surroundings, a foundational dissociation. Lured away from my existence, I thought those around me wanted me to disappear—that I was preferred as an illusion.

I was unable to work for a while. The therapist suggested the break, as did my parents. Acting was the last thing I wanted to do anyhow. Too fragile and erratic, loud noises made me jump. A soft touch on the shoulder could make me cower. The thought of being away, of being alone—for the first time, it all felt impossible. I'd ached to be on my own in the past, and now I'd cling to whatever I could grasp. Any inkling of care I could sense.

For the most part I followed the eating schedule from the therapist. The stress at mealtimes did not go away and knowing how dangerous the situation had become only added to my anxiety. I wanted the external concern to stop. Tired of "the talks" and the scrutiny. And there was a part I desperately wanted at the time, the role of a pregnant teenager no less. I focused on *Juno,* and avoided the core of the issue.

Snacks had been a void in my life, something before bed, unthinkable, but I'd force it down. My weight began to rise. I drank smoothies with blueberries and avocado and protein powder that made me gassy. I was managing the snacks, slowly training my body to chew and swallow and digest food again. To stay calm, to not have to get drunk first. Not ideal, but at least some pounds were returning.

I had to travel to Los Angeles for my final *Juno* audition, which was more of a screen test. I am the first to admit when I am not right for something, but this was one of those rare occasions where by page five, I couldn't fathom not doing it, I just *knew*. I read Diablo Cody's screenplay on the floor of my bedroom in Halifax. Her wit opened up a new vernacular—it was organic and honest. I'd been craving something like this, a character like this, as an actor and an audience member. This I could do.

Still too thin, but much better, I flew to LA with my mother. I had gone from being independent very young, moving out at sixteen, to a kid with their mother traveling alongside them. The thought of functioning alone felt too risky, and I could not take any chances. A suggestion from the well-meaning therapist that I don't think was the best decision. As I grew more confident in my queerness, her denial grew, too.

Before she was a teacher my mom worked for Air Canada, not

as a flight attendant but as a passenger agent. My mother has been forever terrified of flying. For the takeoff, she closes her eyes and braces tight. Turbulence and you witness her heart jump, a sort of shiver runs through the body. I let her know that it's okay, it'll pass. It wrenches my heart watching my mother afraid, a window to her pain. She's had a lot of that in her life.

We reached altitude. My anxiety was fluttering. On a plane you have no choice but to sit, body pressed into the seat, nowhere to flee. I obsessively went over the pages for the audition. Running the dialogue in my head, I wrote it out over and over, a process that helps me remember. My mother finally calmed and focused on a movie.

We flew from Halifax to Toronto, where we met Michael Cera and his father on our Los Angeles flight. For this audition, I was to read thirty pages of the script, mostly with Michael, the lengthiest audition I have ever done. But having just binged *Arrested Development,* I was stoked, his humor original and grounded, emotions on his sleeve. We sat in the middle of the plane, Michael and his father were on the other side of the aisle. We exchanged pleasantries, he was quiet but exuded kindliness.

After takeoff, Michael promptly lowered the meal tray, crossed his arms over it, and rested his head to sleep. He stayed that way until we started our descent. I looked on in admiration and disbelief. How could he be so relaxed? I pressed back my seat, reclining it more, I could see my mom's anxious knees bounce.

Even though it was implied the role was mine before the screen test, my heart still burst with excitement when I got the call. One of those rare occasions—a character who filled me with joy. I'd been cast, a dream role.

Initially we were supposed to make the film a couple months

after the screen test, but it ended up being pushed, which was good, more time to recover, no excuses. Drastically better with food, albeit still self-restricting, work helped me. Being on this set was healing, flashes of torture not following me home, and I was making a point to fuel my body. Not perfect, but a hell of a lot better. I had something meaningful to focus on after feeling unequivocally no meaning at all. Depression had sucked me dry.

It was a job where I felt comfortable, able to start from a grounded place, versus outside my body, trying to crawl back in. Hair, wardrobe, and makeup at work was typically a nightmare for me. Ironically, playing a pregnant teenager was one of the first times I felt a modicum of autonomy on set. I was wearing a fake belly but not being hyperfeminized. For me, *Juno* was emblematic of what could be possible, a space beyond the binary.

While filming in Vancouver I stayed at the Sutton Place, or the "Slutton Place" as some in the industry refer to it. A cavernous hotel, with dated decor, it's located in downtown Vancouver and has long-stay units where actors frequently reside.

My mother and I shared a two-bedroom suite. And her being the daughter of an Anglican minister born in 1954 in Saint John, New Brunswick, well, it made it complicated when I met someone, the first woman I had a suitably consensual sexual relationship with.

I was taken aback the moment I saw Olivia Thirlby. Embodied and bold, her long brown hair moved in slow motion. We were the same age, but she seemed so much older, capable, and centered. Sexually open, far removed from where I was at the time. But the chemistry was palpable, it pulled me in. I was embarrassingly shy with Olivia. She had much more experience. I was closed off. It was rare I let anything in, but I felt comfortable with her, and I began to poke my head out of its shell. We became friends quickly, spending a lot of time together.

We stood in her hotel room. Billie Holiday played. She was about to start making lunch, when she looked directly at me and said point-blank, "I'm really attracted to you."

"Uh, I'm really attracted to you, too."

At that we started sucking face. It was on.

I had an all-encompassing desire for her, she made me want in a way that was new, hopeful. It was one of the first times someone would make me cum, the first time I would open up. And we started having sex all the time: her hotel room, in our trailers at work, once in a tiny, private room in a restaurant. *What were we thinking?* We thought we were subtle. Being intimate with Olivia helped my shame dissipate. I didn't see a glint of it in her eyes and I wanted that—done feeling wretched about who I am.

I do not know if my mom suspected anything. She probably just thought Olivia and I had become fast pals. Which was true. But still, I kept it hidden. Olivia came to my suite maybe once.

We would sometimes hang out in Michael's room, and once Jonah Hill came to visit. It was after they had made *Superbad* but before it had come out. There was weed and gin. Michael had a groovy little keyboard out and was tinkering around with Jonah. He would make music when he wasn't filming, just always being perfectly, annoyingly cool. We all got baked and wandered Vancouver together. We trekked down to Stanley Park, a massive, jaw-dropping green oasis. The gargantuan trees bring you to your knees. The Douglas firs, the western red cedars . . . some towering up to 249 feet. All of these moments brand-new adventures.

Making *Juno* reinvigorated me, inspired me, strengthened me.

We said our sad goodbyes in a curling rink, a very Canadian wrap party. My heart hurt as I traveled home. Switching planes in Toronto, I boarded a flight back to Halifax. Listening to the Moldy Peaches as we broke through the clouds on our descent. I stared out the window, nothing but trees and lakes and rivers below.

What will happen with that little indie? I wondered as the flight landed on the tarmac. The sudden lurch caused me to jump.

11

ONLY KIDDING

———

I did not vomit from the age of eleven until I was twenty-eight, a few months after I came out as gay. At a party at a friend's house in Brooklyn on July Fourth, we climbed up to the roof to watch the fireworks. BANG! POP! I looked to the sky, out over the river the colors exploded across the backdrop, the moon staring down quizzically at us funny humans and our funny things. I became light-headed and my ears started to ring.

Am I really about to vomit? I thought. *Is this the moment my streak is over, like that episode in* Seinfeld *with the cookie?*

Mescal and dessert flew out of my mouth, landing all over my chest.

My inability to vomit until then always felt poignant. Eleven was the age I sensed a shift from boy to girl without my consent. As an adult, I would say, "I just want to be a ten-year-old boy," whenever dysphoria belted out its annoying song, a pop hit that you know the words to and don't know why. It's hard to explain gender dysphoria to people who don't experience it. It's an awful voice in the back of your head, you assume everyone else hears it, but they don't.

Eleven was when I last felt present in my flesh, not suspended above, transient and frantic to return. It was a departure of sorts, a path to a false identity in a shell of a disguise, entering witness protection. He'd seen too much.

I broke it apart slowly, cracking the nuanced layers to rebuild, only to shatter it all again. That pop song remained on loop for more than two decades. Now I hear it seldomly, startling me on shuffle. I've forgotten most of the words, thank God.

My inability to vomit did not mean that I didn't get sick. When I was fourteen I became severely ill with food poisoning the day before a Nova Scotia Provincial Soccer practice. I rushed to the toilet at my father's house. Shitting my brains out, I rested my head on a small, decorative hand towel that dangled on the wall. Fading in and out of reality, as if I could be sucked right out of it, flushed away. E. coli had recently been in the news, mass recalls of produce and meat, and I wondered if I had it.

Eventually my body stopped expelling excrement, and I placed my hand on the counter and lifted myself to standing. One step. Two steps. In the mirror was another face, empty and pale, barely a person. My vision blurred. Light-headed, I left the bathroom, turning off the light as the world went sideways, complete darkness and then, SLAM! I fainted, collapsing hard, my jaw and chin taking the bulk of the impact, jolting my brain. Only a few feet from Dennis and Linda's room. I didn't ask for help, I didn't call for my dad. I did not want to be reprimanded for having disturbed their slumber, or eating whatever I shouldn't have eaten.

My head pounding, I crawled back to my room, and as I was pulling myself up into the bed, Linda came to the door. She must have heard the thump. She was alone.

"What are you doing?" she said with a cold laugh. She left to get me a cool cloth and a bucket when I sputtered in response.

The next morning my mother insisted I still go to soccer. When you play for the provincial team, every practice is a tryout. They overstack the team with the best players in Nova Scotia, and you can be booted at any time. Attendance crucial, soccer was more important than anything. Perhaps my mother exhaled a sigh of relief seeing me run with all the girls.

Sixteen was my soccer number. My favorite number. Only in adulthood have I realized its connection to the date I returned to my mother's for the second half of every month. At first, going over to Linda's had been, between Nintendo and playing with my stepbrother, for the most part fun. But that was different from living together, where her antipathy toward me seemed to grow. I felt her annoyance at this burden from her husband's first marriage. She could get away with it. I never actually talked to my father about how she treated me until I was an adult and I never, not once, stood up to her. I suppose I felt I deserved it, and why the hell wouldn't I? My father knew and did nothing about it.

"Ninety percent of our fights were about you," my father told me many years later, claiming that he *did* protect me and I just wasn't privy to it.

My guess is Linda was not the only one who resented me. I felt that my father did, too. It seems like he was annoyed he had made a baby in the eleventh hour with someone he didn't desire to be with, a puny human, relentlessly keeping the cord strong and taut.

I didn't like growing up in that house. Anything that forced me back home as an adult caused my anxiety to spread like a brushfire, chest aflame. I'd try to surround it with large rocks, like the ring around the bonfire at my father's cabin, firm and solid, unflinching. Instead, my body betrayed me, energy abuzzin'. Pulse rate rising, I'd overcompensate, sparing no effort to buoy up, to hide the hiding, cutting a rug three centimeters above the floor, eggshells everywhere.

The scent of my childhood home, hitting me on the way in, made me nauseated. Taking off my shoes, yelling "hi!" up the stairs, wanting to turn around, no desire to linger long enough to know the why of it all.

They'd all tease me together. "Skid mark" was a nickname Linda coined. We were all at the cabin my dad's father built along Sable River in the early 1980s. It was in a small clearing, nearly a kilometer into the middle of the woods. There is no other structure in sight, aside from the outhouse. No running water or electricity, you collect water from a well with a silver bucket attached to a thin yellow piece of rope that echoes loudly when it meets the surface down below.

The cabin sits close to a family of beavers, their impressive lodge constructed of mud and sticks. The old winding river swerves and snakes its way through a massive meadow until morphing into a narrow, straight stretch. The current accelerates, small rapids muscle through the dam assembled by the family of beavers. Playing in the forest, I'd stumble upon evidence, their teeth having gnawed through a yellow birch.

Only once did I see a beaver fully out of the water. Sitting on the "swimming rock," my siblings and I looked across the river as the beaver climbed onto the shore. The body, taller and thicker than I imagined, held up by its short back legs and webbed, wide feet that resembled the hands of the Babadook. Beavers can weigh up to seventy pounds, reaching about four feet in length, the largest rodents in North America. It would have been bigger than me at that point.

I observed them for my entire childhood, their bodies appearing at dusk, smooth in the river. Their large, powerful, flat tails slapped the water. An echoing force. The beavers claiming their place. Swimming in the river, the color a dark brown with a tint of yellow, like English breakfast tea . . . THWACK! Panicking, I'd dog-paddle to shore, frightened my leg would suddenly snap. Their strong, chiseling teeth clamping, snapping my femur like the birch. They can munch through an eight-foot tree in five minutes.

The cabin is tiny, two stories, everything wood. The kitchen had a little chrome table. The woodstove stood in the center of the cabin between the kitchen and the small couch and two chairs that sat in front of the windows that look out toward the meadow. Knees on the couch, elbows on the windowsill, I would watch deer trot through the grass. And one time only, off in the far distance . . .

"Bear!" Dennis and Linda yelled from the little upstairs balcony off their room.

I raced to the glass with Scott and Ashley, and there it was, running and bouncing, almost a dance. A reminder that we are the scary ones.

Chilling together in the living room, my stepmom would get a look, picking out things I did wrong or embarrassing, and flinging it on a canvas to show. Sort of like all the abstract art she made when I got older and gave to us as gifts.

"Skid Mark," Linda would say, and they would laugh. Calling me the name together, like bullies. The nickname was obvious: birthed from skid marks in my underwear. I'd disassociate, go quiet, just let it happen.

I remember this particular instance because I removed myself and quietly slunk up the pull-down ladder. The piercing sounds from the hinges that needed WD-40 humiliated me further, as if my fault, all that noise. My ears filled with their giggles, causing my shoulders to slump more.

I lay down on the futon where I slept. Crawling into my sleeping bag, I turned to face where the slanted roof met the floor. I closed my eyes and started to cry, soft enough so they could not hear. I never watched this happen to my stepbrother or stepsister—they never had the entire family, all of *us,* focused in and picking on them, making them feel ashamed to the extent that their little body rose and exited the room. A tiny parade of hurt.

Thunks and squeaks from the ladder, I cringed as my dad came and sat next to me on the floor. He put his hand on my spine, I felt my insides retreat.

"We are just kidding around," he said, whispering, rubbing my back. "It's just a joke."

No sorry. Never a sorry. No stop. Never an "Are you okay?"

"I know," I said, masking my sniffles, making the words sound like a smile.

As I got older, I did not want to go to Dennis and Linda when I was in pain or afraid, any negative or disruptive emotion that veered from my usual "happy" self, a performance in its own.

I would shove it back down. As I held my breath, it would leak into my stomach, finding a place to rest.

In the late 1990s, I loved to Rollerblade around Regatta Point.

"What's the hardest part of Rollerblading?"

"Telling your parents you are gay."

Is it bad I love that joke?

I'd take a left from the driveway, head down Spinnaker. Pumping my legs, parallel to the park, alone with the raspy caw caw caws, backup courtesy of seagulls, the crows serenaded me. The tinkling bells from the docked, swaying boats, performed as chimes.

I'd pass the Explosion Memorial on the right, the anchor always there, always waiting. I'd turn on Anchor Drive, passing the town houses on the left and rounding the block back to Spinnaker. I enjoyed the speed, the fantasies, outdoor private play. A spy escaping the enemy. A boy racing to his true love. Olympics for the gold.

Spinnaker Drive begins flat and steady, then curves and begins its decline. Thrilling enough without being too fearsome, I loved zooming down the hill. One day I lost my footing, or perhaps a rock caught in my wheels, small enough not to see but big enough to send me flying. I didn't manage to turn, or stop, and I ran into the curb full-throttle. My feet went in opposite directions as I hit the ground. Stretching, tearing, the hurt unparalleled. Pain radiating out from my groin. When I opened my mouth, guttural sounds I'd never heard before flooded out, ripping through my body. Cavernous, animalistic, from somewhere beneath the vocal cords.

I went into shock, the body a loyal protector. I attempted to rise but couldn't. It was a quiet neighborhood and no one was out. A searing pain shot through my legs as I tried to stand, and I sunk back down. I crawled toward the house, slowly making my way, my bare knees digging into the concrete.

I reached the house and made my way up the driveway to the door. The only person home was Linda. Fear swirled in my belly—I didn't want to need her in this moment.

I struggled out of my Rollerblades. I was silent now, frigid, my body blank. I snailed my way upstairs, not wanting to be seen or heard. Reaching the second floor, I took a tight turn to head to the third. Linda was in the kitchen, preparing food. I didn't say a word, neither did she. When I made it to my room and closed the door, I realized my pants were wet, my crotch utterly drenched. I lowered my pants to see my underwear beet red, the cotton sodden with blood. Panicking, my hands shook as I carefully removed them, brushstrokes from my bloodstained panties leaving evidence on my thighs. The white undies now a dark velvet.

My breaths were short, *just* managing to accomplish the in and out. I went to the bathroom and wiped myself. I left the crimson drawers and went down to the kitchen.

"Linda?"

A pause.

"Yeah?" she said with that tone, her constant aggravation with me.

My mind had left my body, my mouth on autopilot. "I fell Roller-blading and there is blood in my underwear." I kept it simple.

She shrugged. My throat froze, afraid to be admonished, unable to force out more words. As if hypnotized, I went back upstairs. But staring at the evidence, I knew this wasn't insignificant. I returned with the underwear to show her. She stood in the kitchen between the island and the oven. I held them up with both hands. I can still see her face when she saw them, her eyes big and wide, an uncontrollable reaction to the grotesque quality of a kid's underwear soaked in blood.

She snapped into gear, reaching for the phone to call my father, who was thankfully already on his way home. We piled into the car and headed to a nearby clinic. I sat in the back seat and watched as they exchanged panicked whispers, with an intermittent look back at me, then back to the road.

A doctor with long brown hair greeted me kindly, moving quickly but maintaining a sense of calm. I had slipped into a dream, hovering, disassociated, feeling faint. Alone with the doctor, I lay on the examination table, the top of my body covered, the bottom bare. Her gloved hands moved as she spoke to me, talking me through what was next while I looked up at the lights on the ceiling, then back to her, slightly blurred, my eyes adjusting. She started to stick her finger inside my vagina, it made me clench my jaw and tense, halting my breath. She explained what had happened in detail, but all I remember is the words "torn something," and the cold realization that that something was inside of me. Luckily, the tear was *just* small enough that it could be repaired with a dissolvable adhesive tape to avoid stitches. She finished up, and I was returned to Dennis and Linda in a daze.

Years after, I was concerned that something was wrong with my vagina, conceivably due to this incident. The thought originally came at sixteen while I was dating a lovely boy named Kenneth. We met in grade ten at Queen Elizabeth High School in Halifax.

Kenneth played the guitar and was in a band. They'd play at the Pavilion, a music venue on the commons that had all-ages shows, mostly punk concerts. Moshing, a pit overflowing with pubescent pheromones. His house was a fifteen-minute or so walk from school. He'd practice with his band in the basement, his brother, Skyler, on drums. I found it far too loud but acted like I didn't, secretly desperate to be cool.

Kenneth was sweet, sensitive, and cute. A unique face, with prominent cheekbones and electric eyes, his hair dark brown and floppy. I was at his place mostly. His mom, whom I really liked, wasn't often home, and if she was, she didn't care what we were doing. She was warm and spoke to each of us like we were actual human beings rather than just teenagers. It was so easy for adults to forget the fullness of our experience.

We'd fool around upstairs. I didn't really like it, but I didn't mind it either. The kissing, meh. The dry humping, all right. I would pretend to cum, not that Kenneth wasn't or wouldn't be fantastic in bed, I am certain he would be a selfless and generous lover. When we tried to have sex, his dick just would not go in. That whole "wet" thing wasn't happening. We'd try and then stop, try and then stop, try and then stop, and then we stopped trying. I was lucky it was with someone as lovely as him, it could have ended a different way.

I had this idea that something had happened to my vagina during the Rollerblade incident, causing my body to refuse entry. Everyone was talking about "doing it" and "hooking up" and "virginity" and "cum," and I didn't get it. Was everyone also pretending?

I avoided sex with guys and suppressed my real, unrequited crushes. My brain could not comprehend that I simply wasn't interested, that I just didn't want to go through with it, which would be a completely appropriate feeling and response.

When I walked into a gynecologist's office for the first time and recapped the situation, the doctor thought it best to give me my first examination and Pap smear. A med student in residence flanked her, shadowing and observing the process. Legs up, spread wide, the cold metal speculum stretched me open, separating the inside of my vagina. The feeling sent sparks through me, up my pelvis, into my gut, fear mixed with exhilaration. Not pain, just a new discomfort for an unaccustomed body. She dug around in there, the newfangled sensation causing me to fidget. Squirm then stiff, squirm then stiff.

She assured me there was nothing wrong with my vagina. All clear. The response was frustrating at the time—now I had nothing to blame. I sat up and covered my vagina, thinking, *Perhaps if I have sex enough I'll convince myself I enjoy it?*

As my inaugural gynecologist visit was coming to a close, the med student looked at me.

"I really liked you in *Hard Candy*," she said.

I squeezed a smile through a cringe, said thank you and goodbye, and left.

12

ROLLER DERBY

When I went to my first Oscars in 2008 for *Juno,* I could feel how close I was. Not to winning the award, but to the end of the months-long process of campaigning for it. All the parties to attend, the interviews where I smiled, altered my body language and voice, playing along with the role that had been chosen for me. I wanted it to be over, and not just this chapter, but acting altogether.

After awards season concluded, I was supposed to make a film in England. It was based on a famous book, and I was attached as the main character, a sought-after role. Every time the project came up, my agents excitedly spoke of the opportunity, sharing updates and new casting ideas. I would imagine myself in a woman's costume from the mid-nineteenth century. The dress, the shoes, the hair, flashed before my eyes. It was too much after having put on the mask for awards season. I understood that if I were to do it, I would want to kill myself.

It wasn't easy to explain to my reps that I couldn't take on a role because of clothing. A face would scrunch up and tilt sideways, *but you're an actor?* Wardrobe fittings for films ripped at my insides, talons gashing my organs. Fittings for photo shoots and premieres . . . I would nosedive, spiraling into a deep depression, anxiety boisterous. The writhing that ensued surpassed language, and the negligible amount that I was able to communicate only reinforced the gaslighting, that tone of voice. Was it pity?

Clothes leeched to my thighs, my chest, latching fast like a slap bracelet from the 1990s. I cringed at the way people lit up when seeing me in feminine clothing, as if I had accomplished a miraculous feat. I will never forget the faces of glee when I donned a tight gold dress in Cannes for the premiere of *X-Men 3*.

"But you look so beautiful."

"Just play the game."

It was too much to play a role on-screen when the role I played in my personal life was suffocating me already. I pushed myself to dispel the truth for fear of banishment, but I was despondent, trapped in a dismal disguise. An empty, aimless shell. And as usual, I would take it out on myself, obsessing about food, striking my head with my fist. As if pounding my skull would knock it out, the invisible force that stalked me.

I ended up backing out of the film.

Instead, I nabbed the role of Bliss Cavendar in Drew Barrymore's directorial debut, *Whip It,* about a seventeen-year-old from a small town in Texas who falls in love with Roller Derby. Ill fit for the expectations of her mother—played by genius Marcia Gay Harden—and forced to be in beauty pageants her entire childhood, Bliss dreams of getting out. She lies to her parents and joins a Roller Derby team. The Derby world embraces her, supports her, and encourages Babe Ruthless, Bliss's Derby name, to be herself, *to be her own hero,* as Maggie Mayhem, played by the brilliant Kristen Wiig, suggests.

I identified with Bliss, and my aversion to the gloss of Hollywood was no match for the affinity between a closeted queer and the chance to learn Roller Derby. Not being on camera or in a makeup trailer for months and getting to learn a new, dynamic sport was a lifeline. I'd always been an athlete but had lost a lot of that strength. I wanted that again, that physicality, I missed it from my life.

Learning Roller Derby was no joke though. My Derby coach, Axles of Evil—Alex Cohen, famed NPR host—was warm and encouraging, but she was tough as nails. We trained in the former location of the LA Derby Dolls. A large old factory, with a white-brick exterior. The sound of our falls would ricochet around the cavernous inside. I'd done my share of obligatory ice-skating growing up in Canada, and I hoped it, mixed with my Rollerblade years, would translate. It did, at least for the most part. The track was banked, and even getting on and off it was a challenge at first. I buzzed as I pictured us soaring down and around and up and back while being hip checked, or tripped, or barreled to the ground. I was in for it.

I was still dating Paula at the time, and the thought of being apart for such an extended period was agonizing. I would spend the spring learning Roller Derby and then travel to Michigan to make the film throughout the summer. Paula was living in Nova Scotia, not able to come visit me such a long distance away on a whim. I'd be going nonstop in Los Angeles, working with a physical trainer five days a week and with Axles for three days of the week. Quick trips home wouldn't be a reality. Traveling extensively for short visits only ever seemed to increase my loneliness, stress, and sadness.

Los Angeles was still a fairly new landscape, and I felt perpetually stuck. The aloneness I experienced during those *Juno* award months haunted me, a smidgen of the feeling could stir panic. I

went from a person who craved being on my own to someone petri-
fied of it. It was humiliating. I'd made it so far and now here I was,
incomplete and unable to function.

Paula and I decided she should come live in LA while I trained.
We had been in a relationship for a year, lived together in Halifax,
and did not want to manage the distance of it all over again. She
would work as my assistant so she wasn't losing income, driving me
to training in the day, picking me up after. She'd return to Nova Scotia at the end of the summer. We had a dog named Patti at the time,
a brown-and-white Chihuahua that Paula would take on reluctant
walks while I trained. Patti was not a fan of this world, wanting
nothing to do with anyone other than Paula or me. She was content
to live life snuggled on our laps in perpetuity, snarling at anyone who
drew near. We loved her, but she clearly had a past. With Paula as
my assistant we'd operate in the world with no one being the wiser.

We can keep it a secret and still be together. We'll make it work. I
tried to convince myself.

We stayed in a ridiculous house on a hill just north of Hollywood near the 101. It was like nowhere either of us had lived. It was
an architectural folly, all risks and shapes—bold and modern with
that sheeny look, a *Dwell* magazine spread. A movie about a closeted couple coming to Hollywood and the location was impeccable,
now the drama just needed to unfold.

I went from flying around the Derby track to struggling to mo-
tivate at home. A paragraph in a book was difficult to get through.
Nothing I had enjoyed before stimulated me. I'd pretend, but, in
reality, I felt dead inside. I was overwhelmed at being known overnight, recognized constantly. I hated it. People coming up, chipper
and pumped to meet Juno, me wanting to hide in a hole and never
come out. Paparazzi were outside the vet when we were leaving with

Patti, who had gotten very sick. They'd follow us into Whole Foods. Another time, a woman in a white Honda trailed us for almost the whole day taking photos. It always left that lingering, anxious thought, *Can they tell we are together?* I never wanted to leave the house, and Paula was stuck with me, she didn't know anyone in LA.

Paula resented me for being so closeted here. And during our fights I couldn't help but get defensive and bring up that she wasn't out to her family. It didn't seem fair, me having to deal with the bulk of the blame. I was at least trying to make things work, figure out a way for us to be together. In Nova Scotia, even though we were living in the same one-bedroom apartment, her parents did not think we were a couple. And it wasn't like we weren't around them. I was over there all the time. Her mom and dad were very nice, but they were also very homophobic. They were religious, and things don't evolve overnight, especially when the Bible comes into play. And yes, my mom *knew*, but she was disappointed, and that sorrow sprang from the same holy source. But eventually my mom started to change, her old narratives began to crumble, creating space for new ones. When I came out as gay, Paula showed her parents my speech at the Human Rights Campaign conference. Her father got up and left the room and Paula's mother looked to her and asked, "Did you know Ellen was gay?"

In LA, we fought about who was closeting who the most. But, the truth is, it was worse for Paula. I was in denial, desperate to make it work. The family thing was somewhat manageable, albeit hurtful. The Hollywood ball game was a whole other story, riddled with confusing rules that constantly changed. And I had changed. I was different here, she wasn't. I was being told to lie and hide. It puzzled me to watch cis straight actors play queer and trans characters and be revered. Nominations, wins, people exclaiming, "How brave!"

"Keep your personal life private, that is what I tell *all* my clients," my manager would instruct me, while the same clients walked the red carpet with a spouse or came out as heterosexual in an interview. Being arm in arm walking down the street in paparazzi photos was a natural phenomenon, even encouraged for publicity. There was always the pressure to appear more feminine—dresses to events, high heels, "take off your hat." This was my manager's attempt at helping me build my career. In her heart she was caring for me, coaching me to morph into part of the club, making sure I still had all opportunities available to me. I got lost in the part, unable to fully lean into the character but still losing track of myself. Stuck in the liminal space.

Hollywood is built on leveraging queerness. Tucking it away when needed, pulling it out when beneficial, while patting themselves on the back. Hollywood doesn't lead the way, it responds, it follows, slowly and far behind. The depth of that closet, the trove of secrets buried, indifferent to the consequences. I was punished for being queer while I watched others be protected and celebrated, who gleefully abused people in the wide open.

"The system is twisted so that the cruelty looks normative and regular and the desire to address and overturn it looks strange," Sarah Schulman writes in her required read, *Ties That Bind: Familial Homophobia and Its Consequences.*

Paula's and my relationship was caught in the cross fire, and I was losing track of how to make it work.

Being closeted while learning Roller Derby has a special type of irony to it, given how intertwined queerness is with the sport, but throwing myself into learning this new skill still opened up a much-needed pocket of joy in my life at the time.

Drew was also learning to Roller Derby when she wasn't in preproduction for the film, and we had a blast together. More people had joined, the sensational Zoë Bell, who learned to Roller Derby in what felt like five minutes. She was fearless and full of fun, her energy always joyous and generous. We sped around the track, racing and bumping and laughing and falling and getting back up. It was actually the falling that eased the trepidation. You have a few big crashes, realize it is not a big deal, the pads work, you got this.

Juliette Lewis came aboard, Eve and Kristen Wiig soon after. Everyone worked hard. All of us equally focused and supportive. Learning something new together, especially something as challenging as Derby, allowed us to bond quickly. It created a palpable chemistry, clear in the film. It was such an awesome group. I am grateful for those times.

When we were capable enough, actual Derby Dolls would join our sessions, adding more bodies to experience the sensation of an actual jam. Scrimmaging with them was terrifying. The first time real-life Derby stars came to practice with us, my hands trembled as I tied my skates. Making my way around that track had been hard enough, and now women twice my size were coming at me with their hip bones. I hoped my helmet and mouth guard were doing enough to hide my terror. There was no time to think. We swerved and smashed and as the nerves dissipated, exhilaration took the reins. Playing with them improved my abilities dramatically. The moment when you commit to trust your feet, no more looking down, head up, that is when you really start flowing. Shifting from thought to instinct. What a special opportunity to tackle fears alongside others—something I wasn't so familiar with at the time—witnessing the work pay off and the camaraderie form. But despite that closeness and the trust, it would be a while before I shared that Paula was more than my friend and assistant. Not that they couldn't already tell.

We moved to Michigan at the start of the summer to make the film. It took place in Texas but was shot predominantly in Detroit, Ann Arbor, Ypsilanti, and Frankenmuth, with just a day or two in Austin, Texas.

More people were cast, and the training continued. The days would begin with alternating yoga and calisthenics classes. It was intimate, all of us fully committed, laughing, tired, but having fun. However, I did feel inherently dissimilar, perhaps reminding me of the high school soccer days? Not just mismatched physically, but also energetically. Despite always being invited in, I buzzed around the fringes, unable to wholly connect.

When we'd been filming on skates all day and losing our heads from exhaustion, Kristen and I would work between takes on a musical we had spontaneously created called *The Unidentified Beast*. It was based on an article we saw online about an unknown creature that had washed ashore in Montauk. It was referred to as "the unidentified beast." We'd gesture dramatically as we skated, choreography revealing itself through our emotion. We'd improvise songs as we looped around, delusional with fatigue. Our main go-to line was pretty straightforward: "The Unidentified Beaaaaassssssttttttt!" we'd belt, arms raised. It didn't get old. At least for us, perhaps the surrounding cast and crew felt different.

We haven't always kept in touch, but at certain, significant moments, when I really needed someone, Kristen was always there. She lights everything up. The first time I began communicating how I wasn't okay to LA pals was to Kristen and Alia Shawkat, who plays Bliss's best friend, Pash. It came out accidentally, the words just jumped out. I was huddled with them at a party at Drew's house in Hollywood, many months after we had wrapped the film.

We stood chatting. They were speaking excitedly. I felt lost in space, disassociated. It was a period where I almost never left my apartment, and even in the apartment I could not operate. The TV would be on, I'd lie on the couch, but not watching it. I'd fixate on food. I felt too afraid to text a friend to make a plan, as if my presence was an endless burden. I was sinking in slow motion, like a nightmare where you go to scream but nothing comes out. Mouth wide, lips parting, wanting it, you try again . . . silence. And down you go.

I looked at these two wonderful people. I'd met Alia when I read off camera for her audition. Already a major fan, having watched all of *Arrested Development,* I was even more blown away by her in person. Sincere, risk-taking, and naturally comical, she made it seem effortless. Our chemistry sparked, immediately playful and free. Alia became one of my best friends in real life, too.

"I'm miserable." It was as if someone else had said it. A new guest over my shoulder.

"What?" they said, attention shifting to me.

And it came out. I was hurting, the closet too much, my relationship crumbling, I couldn't leave my home. I believed it unattainable to ever be out. Unthinkable the idea I could be where I am now. I would have laughed and dismissed the suggestion altogether, that this would be a feasible future for me. I'm not precisely sure why my feelings emerged in that moment. I do know I trusted them, felt cared for and protected, I knew they'd never judge me. Kristen and Alia were people I could be myself around, or at least work toward it with. They supported my truth, helping me shovel out the bullshit that covered it, wanting me to feel free. But despite people's desire to help, it would all take me so long. False ends and false starts, me fooling myself, justifying suppression and self-harm. Rewarded for lying and punished for sharing the secret.

"You can make a choice and go or stay. But this is my reality, my life, I'll never be able to be out. I don't know what else to say," I said to Paula in my studio apartment in Hancock Park, my first place in Los Angeles after making the official move.

I really believed this. And a couple years later, I still felt the same.

The anxiety never stopped. Pounds were dropping, panic attacks were preventing me from leaving the house. Many days I felt myself unsafe to drive. My lack of motivation alarming, my desire for nothing too big. It was my manager who got me to my first real therapist, a lifesaving introduction.

"We need to get you to a place where you can come out," a new therapist said to me when I was twenty-three.

"No, that is impossible," I replied without thought. It moved through my lips as organically as my queer walk.

When the topic of gender came up, I could not speak, I would just weep. It was too hot to touch. It would take another decade before I properly addressed it, until I was able to sit with myself long enough to listen. Until I was pushed so far that I didn't have a choice. The last fork in the road.

13

BUCKETS

———

As the shoot for *Whip It* was coming to a close, the thought of bursting this bubble and going back to Los Angeles with Paula disturbed me. I wanted to get as far away from Hollywood as I could.

I had been fixated on the state of our environment and the catastrophic impact we've had on it. As I became more and more entrenched in Hollywood, I was traveling around the world constantly for work, staying in luxurious hotels, chucking the towels in the tub to be washed.

I searched online for somewhere I could go and learn about sustainable living, wanting to know what it meant for humans to exist in sync with our natural surroundings. I stumbled upon a place outside Eugene, Oregon, called Lost Valley. As described on their site, *Lost Valley is a learning center, educating youth and adults in the practical application of sustainable living skills. We take a holistic approach to sustainability education, engaging students in ecological, social, and personal growth.*

Looking into the various programs, I settled on the Permaculture Design Certificate Course. Paula was planning on coming, too. It would be a month of living and learning in an intentional community, far removed from the world of film, and I could wear whatever I wanted.

A week out from heading to Oregon, Paula decided not to come. She did not want to be away for a month. She'd returned home, and settling in Halifax felt nice for Paula, a coziness, a community and familiarity. She'd been following me around, tagging along, no real agency of her own. Out of a groove she wanted back in.

Now the thought of going to Lost Valley without her filled me with dread. I'd be alone, walking into a situation with complete strangers. Going solo into an unknown situation was one thing, but this new reality I found myself in, where people I had never met knew who I was, added an extra layer of anxiety and discomfort that I wasn't sure I could reconcile. Lost Valley, the course, the space, that time disconnected from my current ways, was something I craved, I wanted to push through my silly little fears and go.

"My keys are always in my pocket, that is what I tell myself," explained Drew. "If I'm not sure, if I'm hesitant and scared, I simply remind myself that I have my keys in my pocket and I can leave at any point. You can just *leave*."

A pretty straightforward suggestion, but one I had not considered. To this day, I will say this to myself, and it still helps.

I flew into Portland, where I changed planes, and continued on to Eugene. I arrived the day before I was to show up at Lost Valley, so I booked a room in a motel. My nerves had calmed somewhat, the travel complete, but stress crept back in, social anxiety mounting even while alone. I plunked down on the bed, the top blanket scratched my elbows. Grabbing the remote, I rolled over and turned on the TV. *E.T.* was on. I grinned and almost winked, as if to say, *I hear you.* I love synchronicity, regardless of what it means, I notice it and roll with it.

E.T. is one of my favorite movies of all time, I even have EP PHONE HOME tattooed on my arm. I probably watch it once a year, and never have I not bawled my eyes out. I wished so badly to be Elliott when I was a little boy. For my first Halloween after I came out as trans, I donned a red hoodie and by chance already had sneakers that looked just like his in the film. I dressed up as Elliott, hit the streets of Manhattan with some pals, and had the best Halloween ever. Wishes can come true.

When I awoke in the motel the next morning the air was moist, fog loitered in silence. I soaked it all in. I did not have very much luggage. After having traveled for a month throughout Eastern Europe with only a backpack, I'd learned how to keep a bag pared down. My cab arrived and I plunked my bag in the back seat and got in.

This was my first time in Oregon. I stared out the window as we sailed down the highway, ever since watching *E.T.* my nerves had thankfully diminished. Passing churches, gas stations, irrigation services, and mechanic shops along the way, it reminded me of Nova Scotia, a certain aesthetic in rural spaces that immediately jolts me home. The driver took a right off the highway onto Rattlesnake Road. We descended into a new world, swallowed into the forest, slaloming through. Trees, all trees, with creeks roaming and meeting and splitting. He took another right onto Lost Valley Lane. I said thank you and goodbye as he dropped me at the foot of the property.

People welcomed me with big smiles and warm eye contact. I was directed to where I would be living, a building that had been the former sleeping quarters of the all-boys summer camp that existed there before. Wooden bunks were separated by thin walls that did not reach the ceiling. Next to the lower bunk was a bedside table, and instead of doors, curtains hung. I unpacked my things, leaving my cell phone off and behind. The washrooms were shared. We did not use toilets to pee, just to poo. Urinating happened in a bucket next to the toilet full of wood shavings (a carbon source) to minimize the smell. When the odor inevitably made its way through, we would take the bucket and dump it on the giant compost outside. Urine is an excellent nitrogen source. You can absolutely compost your shit as well, it's just a tad complicated and takes more planning.

Other students coming to take the class arrived throughout the day. We all introduced ourselves, getting to know each other. People were there from Oregon to Malaysia, from South Korea to Indiana and Nova Scotia. There were about a dozen of us in the course. Lost Valley itself was also a permanent community with a dozen or so people living there at the time. I had never been to an "eco village" before, it was in many ways what I had imagined. Biodiverse, dense gardens curled and reached and overlapped, none of that monoculture business. It produced more food than I could fathom, an abundance from such a compact space. Different plants worked together, looking out for each other. Chickens ran around in their coop, picking at the compost thrown in for them to eat, munching and digging and scratching and pooping until the chicken coop is moved a few yards away to another location, leaving the soil underneath fresh and ripe, closing the loop.

The food at Lost Valley was mostly from the property or nearby. The freshness, the colors, the smells, it was like living in the Halifax Farmers Market. Those vegetables were some of the best I'd ever had. A bite of kabocha squash forced my eyes closed, no words, mouthwatering with the roasted elephant garlic from the yard that I smooshed with my fork . . . the earthy sweet melted in my mouth, filling it. I was patient, it soothed. Nourishing on every level, harvested one hundred feet away. I could feel every cell in my body screaming THANK YOU when I ate that food. Before dinner that initial evening (and every lunch and supper thereafter), all of us would circle the spread of food, hold hands, and close our eyes. Taking a moment, we joined as a group to express our gratitude, our appreciation for one another, for the earth, for how lucky we were to sit down and consume life-giving plants and grains and water. It was a moment to breathe, to connect and ground, to remind ourselves. An easy thing to roll your eyes at, but I really liked it. A similar but different way to say grace. I told myself I would keep up the ritual, but it's unfortunate how easily these types of epiphanies slip away when we are thrust back into society.

I was comfortable. No one seemed to be fazed by the *Juno* business. If anything, I figured they would like me less due to my occupation and therefore would not be interested in it. Hollywood does not exactly go hand in hand with permaculture. But that first evening after we had all eaten and spent time getting to know each other, someone put on music. "Anyone Else but You" by the Moldy Peaches, the song that ends *Juno,* came out of the speakers. I felt a sizzle of embarrassment, unintentionally pressing my eyelids tight. I had wanted so badly to escape it, that time, how people saw me, but perhaps it was needed to break the ice. We spoke of the film briefly, and then of acting for a bit longer, and then that was that, I could just be me, whatever that meant at the time.

The group was full of warm, supportive, and passionate people who cared about Earth and our collective future. I had been mostly dismissed in my friend circle in Los Angeles when I spoke to these issues, or bought books for them that they would never read. They'd giggle at me in the *you're being dramatic* way, when I would discuss resource exploitation, the climate crisis, how quick it was coming, how it would affect the most vulnerable first, how the consequences would be unthinkable, the impending collapse of our society and our role in it.

"I think you're overreacting" was a common response.

"You lesbian hippie," another pal said.

I'd get frustrated, feeling disregarded and dispirited by the lack of concern and empathy. The opulence urged entitlement, and the entitlement required ignorance. But my self-righteousness and judgment were means to alleviate my own guilt, my own life of unnecessary consumption in Los Angeles.

It was invigorating to be at Lost Valley, to be engulfed in such a wealth of conversation, immersed in a common focus, to gain knowledge, to be humbled. I'm lucky for that, most people can't take a month from work and travel to Oregon to take a course.

I always woke up with the sun. Roosters sounded the alarm, a chorus of birds and insects serenaded my hazy rise to consciousness. I slept on the bottom bunk, no one slept above me. Usually one of the first up, I'd get changed and tiptoe down to the bathroom. Squatting, I'd pee in the bucket, maybe I'd need the toilet post-coffee. Washing my hands and my face, no mirror to glare at, a break from that nuisance. Breakfast was the only meal of the day without a group circle before. It let people take their time getting up, have silence if they needed. I enjoyed tucking away somewhere, perhaps the little library, a moment alone with oatmeal and an apple, a little quiet before the chatter. The day began in the classroom mostly. We would cover everything from gray-water systems to water catchment to garden design, composting to medicinal tinctures, fermentation to building a cob hut, and on and on. The amount of information was overwhelming, or rather, it was overwhelming how little I knew. It struck me as sad, *I should already have this knowledge.* Instead, my mind had been shaped and plugged into a system that makes us sick while we make the planet sick.

The reality is that I'd benefited from being plugged in, but learning all this new material felt like I was relinquishing society's hold on me. I'd spent a sizable amount of time squeezing into the system even though my body rejected it. Far removed from myself and the world around me, this grounded me, this gave me hope.

No scarcity complex or illusion of constant linear growth. A true way of observing, of caring and relating to the world. Here was a space with dreams beyond self and ideals that truthfully felt no different from what we'd learned in primary school—be kind, collaborate, take care of the Earth, share—concepts that don't jibe well with our capitalist system, the ones they push us to forget.

We went over the principles of permaculture, a term coined in the 1970s, a result of combining the words "permanent" and "agriculture." The core tenets of cultivating a regenerative, reciprocal relationship with nature are derived from Indigenous science and wisdom. Permaculture illustrates our interconnectedness and how we can live in partnership with the land and natural cycles of our planet. Essentially, slow down, look, listen, and witness what is happening. Let the landscape tell *you* what to do, make meaningful decisions or adjustments, versus forcing your ideas or expectations. Take a breath and find the alignment. Nature takes time, all of our growth does. If we can see the impact of our actions, perhaps we can make better decisions based on those observations. Work *with* the cycles, not against them. Permaculture is about closing the loops. Yield with no waste. Our actions reflecting the planet's. And as humans, how do we as individuals harness and store our energy? How best can we protect it, embrace it, and share it? To keep cycling through?

On the third day, a final person arrived late for the course. He had been at Lost Valley for a month or so right before the course began. I could sense the delight regarding his return. He had originally arrived with a group of WWOOFers, the Worldwide Opportunities on Organic Farms, a grassroots organization that formed in 1971 and connects volunteers with host farms. They had all just traveled across the country from New York City in a biodiesel school bus. He left Lost Valley to stay in Portland with his fellow WWOOFers but chose to say goodbye and head back south to take the permaculture course.

I felt a thread between the two of us. A version of love at first sight when I saw him. Ian was small in stature, big in presence, with an effusive charm and knowing eyes. A beanie sat atop his head, concealing a bun that kept his massive red mane of hair contained; unrestrained, it flowed all the way down to his ass. Gesturing as he spoke, his movements were distinct, frenetic, and full of flair. His vernacular witty, sharp, and spicy. I could not stop laughing. I was drawn to him, something already attached, it would just take a little detangling to get close.

"Want to come with me to Portland this weekend?" I asked on a whim.

We were sitting in the computer room together, researching how people manage to utilize the permaculture principles in densely populated areas. I wanted to seek out and visit examples of urban permaculture. And I also wanted to see a woman I had a crush on.

"Yeah, I'm down," Ian said.

I rented us a white sedan, and off we went. Ian and I barely knew each other, but it did not matter. We existed well together, an unspoken agreement to skip the silly stuff and jump right in.

Our love and friendship was solidified on that trip, an intimacy encouraged if not forced by the car. We hadn't yet begun to know our trauma, but in talking, we were starting to see it. It was the first time I bonded with someone so fiercely who understood a particular shame. We spoke of similarities in our childhoods, families, unrequited loves, hometowns, and although we were part of different systems, something about our upbringings connected us, a roundedness and similar suffering. It was as if we entered a field of pain, yes, but also one of camaraderie and healing. Something altered for me in that time, knowing him. I felt supported and seen, I could put my guard down, relax, here was a true friend.

We were both in a space of needing not only a respite but also new ways to see things. Seeking comfort, yet leaning into our discomfort as well. A risk-taking through wanting rest and a desire for community that was connected to our queerness, digging through the layers to find it. We craved a paradigm shift from other worlds, and required other eyes that didn't hold us down to old narratives.

When we arrived in Portland, our first stop was to meet a woman who had turned her small Craftsman home on a compact property into a permaculture haven. She produced zero trash, and the list of *just* the edible perennials growing in her yard was mind-blowing. She had chickens and rabbits, water catchment and gray-water systems. There was even a silkworm tree. I'd never seen anything like it. She gave us a tour of her house, explaining how she composted her shit. Pee went in one bucket, shit in another, and if I am remembering correctly, she would rotate biannually between two compost bins, closing one off for six months so nature could work its magical chemistry, transforming waste into fresh, fertile soil to grow something new. Her root cellar was filled to the brim, cans upon cans, jars upon jars of preserved food. It was magnificent.

I had never been to Portland before and wasn't sure where we

should stay. This was a perfect excuse to text my crush for sugges-
tions. We checked into a hotel, dropped our backpacks, and lay on
the one queen-size bed. *He's cute,* I thought as I looked at Ian, won-
dering what he was thinking. A sense of attraction, yes, but more a
curiosity. Strange how immediate intimacy often conflates the two.

We went to a wine bar to meet up with her and her partner.
The four of us sat at a high table next to the window. I looked at
my crush from across the table, eyes glued. She was brilliant, funny,
multitalented, and sexy, and I was transfixed by her mouth, had
been since watching the music video for "Entertain" by Sleater-
Kinney compulsively.

I had first met Carrie Brownstein at the *SNL* after-party when
I hosted back in 2008. Sleater-Kinney has always been one of my
favorite bands. After school in grade twelve, before my mom was
home from teaching, I would strip down to my sports bra and briefs,
close the blinds, and place *The Woods* CD in my mother's stereo
system in the living room. I loved the cover—forest grows through
a theater floor, heavy red curtains frame the wooden stage, close
to fully open. Pressing Play, I'd crank it up and up and up. The
moment the drums hit—Janet Weiss, taking you like the tide—my
body would drop, surge, and sway, I'd enter a different world.

> On the day the duck was born
> The fox was watching all along he said
> Land ho!
> Land ho!

Corin Tucker's voice, its otherworldly, guttural bellow, had me
breaking into a full dance, head banging, jumping jacks, mash-up.
Full throttle to the entire record, I'd go nonstop, flailing myself

around the house, all limbs extending, stretching, frantically releasing energy. Sweat dripping, I'd drop to the floor, give twenty, run up the stairs, down the stairs, push-ups again. "Entertain" is my favorite Sleater-Kinney song, Carrie's voice, that singular yowl, it motivated me, sent me somewhere, I felt it in my bones.

> Hey! You look around they are lying to you!
> They are lying, ha, they are lying!
> Can't you see it is just a silly ruse?
> They are lying, I am lying, too!
> And all you want is entertainment,
> Rip me open, it's so freeing, yeah

I did this pretty much every day when I got home from school. I rotated Sleater-Kinney's *The Woods* with Peaches CDs, they were the most actively spun—cute baby queer. Insulated, I had the space to release, force it out of the body, attempting to jostle awake a connection. For lack of a better word, it felt spiritual, the music held me while I pranced freely.

Upstairs, I'd make a pit stop in my mom's room. To the left of her bed was a full-length mirror. I'd stare at myself in my underwear and sports bra, my bangs gooey with perspiration. Turning my body to the right while cranking my head to the left, I'd interrogate my profile, always surprised. Breathing in, it swells, the poor things always suffocated.

Carrie and I became good pals and still are. Our shame at the time bonded us, a recognized pain and internal strife. Our mutual self-loathing bringing us close.

"Every self-respecting person hates themselves," Carrie said once, making me laugh.

Terrified to be out, resentful of the entitled desire to pry open who we were, pushing not only before we were ready, but before we even knew what to say. There's a shared joy in knowing that the love did come. A bond shifting from shame to healing.

I didn't take my eyes off Carrie until I had to. Empty wineglasses sat on the table, I watched her mouth as she took her final sip.

That night, Ian and I slept soundly. Sleeping in the same bed came without issue or awkwardness. The next day, we drove to a small community of people who had been formerly unhoused. Between donations from hardware stores and volunteer engagement, the space appeared to be thriving, with permaculture as one of the main focuses. Wood and supplies would be dropped off and used to build tiny homes. Food grew throughout, water catchment tanks stood tall, compost had its place. We were fortunate to be welcomed in, to have them share the evolution of the community with us, how the principles of permaculture were being utilized.

Ian inspired a new sense of poetry in me, instilling a strength to open the heart, grounding me in ways I didn't know I needed. We discussed art and literature I was not yet familiar with. I wanted to devour information through books, and was always looking for recommendations, from Bill McKibben to David Suzuki to Naomi Klein. In grade twelve I thought I'd go to university and planned on applying to the University of Toronto. I had not been sure what I wanted to study though, my lack of clarity signified I should give it a beat. Cast in *X-Men* a few weeks later, my first job in well over a year, it ended up being the launchpad into working nonstop. I thoroughly enjoyed learning, well, if it was something I had an interest in, if not, I was stubborn. I wanted my ignorance to be revealed, for new perspectives to take the place of the dominant narratives I'd grown up with, rooted in bigotry and white supremacy. Since I did not attend school after graduating, I devoured books, almost always nonfiction. I didn't want to stop growing and expanding, and I was terrified I would. I still strive to grow and remind myself to set my self-righteousness aside, there's always more to learn.

At the end of our trip, we popped into a record store to get a CD for the ride home. They had those listening stations where you could preview new releases. I put on the hip, large headphones to listen to Emilíana Torrini's "Fireheads" from *Me and Armini*.

> Somebody's got a long way to go.
> You're not sitting by the phone no more.
> You're gonna throw it away, crash it on a rock.
> Yeah, so you can live your life.

Is how it begins.

We got in the white Ford and headed back south toward Eugene. Obsessed with that record, her voice, the sounds, trippy and uplifting, interwoven with depth and emotion, fusing beauty with heart-wrench. It became the score of our future trips together, the beginning of a long story. Our weekend adventure to Portland was an understanding and experimentation in how to follow our joint curiosities, how to be a team and creative partners. I think both of us were yearning for a sense of embodiment that we weren't sure we'd ever feel. Though stuck in our individual shame storms, when together, so much more felt possible.

"Bleeder" was the song we listened to the most, the last on the album *Me and Armini*. Her voice washed over us while we curved through the enormous spruce and fir trees, and faded out as we pulled up to Lost Valley, the song coming to an end right before stopping the car. Taking a moment of stillness, reverence, the magic of it all. The intimacy that sharing music brings. I sensed reawakened imagination, a spark. I felt hope.

Meanwhile, communication between Paula and me was falling apart. My fault mostly, I'd stopped calling as much. I blamed it on reception, which was only partially true. Angry, but not sure why, it manifested as passive-aggressive. I felt unburdened by this sense of personal freedom. This was the best that existing had felt in a long, long time. Selfishly, I cared more about my present adventure and new friendship than about taking care of my relationship.

One of my most cherished memories from Lost Valley is a simple one: making sauerkraut. Chopping and chopping a countless number of recently harvested green cabbages with a group of earnest and wholehearted people whose journeys had twisted and turned with pain and joy, trauma and healing, all leading to the now where we found ourselves.

We put the sliced and diced cabbage into large buckets. After adding salt, we began to pound with our fists, over and over and over, pulverizing the diced cabbage, making the liquid separate. Listening to music, connecting, we were making food that would last for months at least. Can it, and it'll last for years. When the moisture rose, hovering *just* above the top of the cabbage, I took a plate, placing it on the surface, it fit like a glove. I added a rock on top to weigh it down. Store it away, let it ferment for a couple weeks, and there you go: sauerkraut. What a sublime way to spend time with people. Purposeful and nourishing.

At the end of the permaculture course they had a little graduation party with a talent show. Ian was voted the MC, which fit his gregarious personality perfectly. He decided to host the evening in drag as Courtney Love and encouraged everyone to join in on the drag theme, and most did. We dug through a chest of costumes, overflowing with dresses and long shirts and a cluster of wigs. Ian covered his long red locks with a frazzled blond wig and wore a white slip that stopped above his knees. I loved watching him, it was sexy and embodied. I dressed up as Kurt Cobain, which I did not need to borrow a costume for, I already wore ripped jeans and white T-shirts and large flannels.

He led the show magnificently, never skipping a beat. The charisma, the sass, we laughed and people shared, vulnerable but willing. Beer and tequila and wine made their way about as people sang songs and read poetry. I played a tune I had written on the guitar, simple but sincere. The tenderness that was in that room was nameless, a bonding with strangers that went beyond amicability. It felt magical.

The next morning, plenty of us haggard from the booze, we stood outside in a circle. We held hands while everyone took a turn to reflect on their time there, to say their goodbyes. I felt calm at first, peaceful and grateful, but then an insatiable amount of sadness consumed my body. I began weeping, snot dripping down my face and chin. I kept wiping it away with my windbreaker. My time at Lost Valley, that was the closest I had felt to me in a long time, where I felt present with anything at all. Don't get me wrong, wherever you are, the mind follows, my brain still taunted me, but fuck, it was a hell of a lot quieter.

Here I found myself again, creeping closer. I felt a new sense of strength, I learned and allowed myself to express my pain a smidgen more. But this was hard to hold on to outside of Lost Valley, no longer in the woods without a mirror, but back in Los Angeles with its relentless traffic and sprawling lawns.

At the party, Ian and I finished with a duet. Sitting in a foldout chair, I picked up the guitar and settled it in my lap. The candlelight lit everyone's faces, illuminating kind and encouraging eyes. I looked to Ian and he looked back, our nerves peeking through. I smiled and he smiled, too, as if to say, *I got you.* We played "Doll Parts." There was video of it at some point, but we have never been able to recover it. How much better, though, it lives in our shared memories, those moments that started it all.

14

U-HAUL

The first time I tried to speak to my mom about sexuality, it didn't go very well. I was fifteen and coming to terms with how attracted I was to women, only letting myself think of them when I was alone.

Searching online: Am I gay?

How do I know if I am gay?

There was no need to avert my eyes from my male peers. They did not titillate me. My nerves hummed around certain girls, I'd have to avoid them. *It must be so obvious,* I'd worry.

I was in the passenger seat, head down, mustering up my strength. I turned to my mother. Her eyes were on the road. Her silver earrings dangled, not quite reaching her jawline, swaying with the car's movement.

"Mom, I think I may be gay—"

"That doesn't exist!" she yelled before I'd completed the word.

My body sank in the passenger seat, the air sucked from me.

I hung my head. She looked forward again and neither of us said another word about it.

As I aged, it became clearer that I wasn't going to be a pretty straight girl. The pressure from my mother to alter my appearance began to increase, alongside the bullying at school. I tried. My mom's joy and relief faded to disappointment as I began to return to my original state.

She did not want me hanging out exclusively with boys anymore.

"You like Tina, why don't you do something with her this weekend?" she'd say offhandedly, as if I didn't know it wasn't simply a casual, friendly question.

When high school began, she encouraged me to spend more time with the girls on my soccer team rather than my closest pals. She didn't want me hanging with the kids who were dressed in all black with various colors of hair, purple, green-blue, poking out from under hoods and beanies. The freaks, the artists . . . let's be real, the queers. At one point, suspecting it was a group of pot smokers (it was), she said I couldn't be around them, despite being aware of the extreme drinking in the jock scene. We didn't *not* drink, but nothing like the popular kids. Anytime I hear Joe Budden's "Pump It Up" I'm transported to 2003, a living room in the South End, drowned in the stench of alcohol and sweat and horniness. Armpit stains taking shape on the American Eagle shirts, girls grinding their asses against the guys, like in the music videos on television. It was unusual when someone *didn't* have to get their stomach pumped.

It always felt more about image than anything. Less about me going to hell and more about my mother's ego. She wanted what the other soccer moms had, a daughter.

I didn't talk to her about my sexuality again until I fell in love with Paula at twenty years old. Actually, I didn't talk about my sexuality even then, I just said, "I'm in love with a woman and her name is Paula."

At twenty-four I tried again. "I'm gay, Mom, you know that, right? I'm gay and I'm not going to end up with a man," I finally said when a woman moved in with me.

I met my second girlfriend right around my twenty-fourth birthday at a surprise birthday party for Drew. It had been two years since Paula and I, unable to make the distance work anymore, had broken up. We immediately clicked, I didn't want to leave her side the whole night, unabashedly following her around. She was so fucking funny, deadpan with a perfect dash of cynicism. Whenever she would disappear from view, I'd find myself searching. Enraptured by her eyes when she smiled, a sexy, almost mischievous smirk. The way she moved her body, an effortless cool. She was queer and confident, an actor whose movies I loved. That was the first time I exchanged numbers with someone.

The night ended in the wee hours of the morning as we closed out the bar. But I was too shy to text, to make a plan. I had yet in my adult life to reach out to a woman like that, to initiate. Time passed, but I could not stop thinking of her. Absent-minded, I'd hold Command and N to search her name in a new window, procrastinating from work to scroll and stare. It was close to a month later and I couldn't muster the courage to simply ask, "Hi, want to grab a bite sometime?" Instead, I used the excuse of a movie premiere to invite her and her best friend, which made it feel less pressured, but just as obvious.

It was the premiere of *Super,* a film I made right after *Inception.* Rainn Wilson stars as a DIY superhero, and I played his "kid sidekick," Libby. When the scene arrived with me in my superhero costume, standing in the doorway trying to get Rainn to fuck me, I cringed. My character stands, stroking her pussy under a little skirt while saying, "It's all gushy," before forcing herself on him. *Fuck,* I thought, regretting both the scene and inviting my crush. Somehow forgetting that this may not be the film you would want a crush to see. Her and her bestie still came to the after-party though. They were sweet and complimentary. I was shaking with nerves, whether they noticed or not, I am not sure.

The day after that we texted, my strategy had worked, albeit rather clumsily. We made a plan for a date but it would not be for a couple weeks, and I was impatient. In another inept move, I convinced Alia Shawkat to have a party for the sole purpose of inviting her. She walked in wearing black jeans, Converse, and a red flannel. The moment I saw her, I lifted, a feeling I hadn't had since Paula. We all played running charades, laughing our asses off, I wanted to impress her so badly. I couldn't screw this up. During a pause in the game, I stood with her in a short and small hallway, a perfect little nook. Our backs leaned against the wall, she moved in close, her shoulder touching mine. We both looked to the floor smiling and pressed the sides of our bodies together.

I fell in love fast and hard. We tried to pace out the dates but quickly were spending almost every night together and on our way to cliché. I lived in Beachwood Canyon at the time, she was in the Valley, a bit of a ride on the 101. My place didn't have much inviting furniture. The living room had a broken futon against the wall with some pillows and two stiff chairs. I literally owned one mug, my fridge was more than likely empty—so we were typically at hers. She had a proper living room with comfortable furniture and a TV in the bedroom. A walk-in closet that was the kind of tidy and organized I could only dream of.

Being with her was the first time I was consistently around a queer group of friends. In high school, there were only whispers of us types, if that, and I was still very, very closeted. Other than the time with Paula at Reflections, and a nerve-racking experience at a bar in Paris with Alia (a story for another book), I had not stepped foot into a gay bar. I was not and had never been a part of a queer community, how to access such a thing was not just a mystery but an impossibility. The loss of which was sizable. Agony in isolation, the shame and pain that I thought was mine alone. My heart aches for my younger self. A tiny bug running to the rim of an upside-down juice glass. What a difference it would have been to sit with queer and trans pals and have them say, *I feel that way, too. I felt that way, too. We don't have to feel that way. You don't have to feel that way.* Not a magic eraser of shame, but it would have undoubtedly quickened things up.

Again, my degree of secrecy suffocated the relationship. It was hard on her, but I was wordless in my excuse other than these five—*sorry, I can't be out.*

I dropped her off at a rehearsal one morning. Pulling up in my silver Mini Cooper, she climbed out onto the Hancock Park curb as I turned down PJ Harvey's "Let England Shake." Her black sunglasses protected her from the already searing sun.

"I love you," she said.

"I love you, too," I replied.

A coworker had witnessed me send her off from the Mini, but my face hadn't been visible. She said it was private after he inquired about the relationship. He joked Minnie Driver was her secret girlfriend, and her coworkers referred to me as that going forward.

She slid her arm around me at a sit-down Bon Iver concert one evening. My body stiff as a board, head still and forward, my eyes danced around, as if they were the ones performing. It felt better to not ask for her arm's removal in order to forgo a night of intense arguing and dramatic hand gestures. The first time I would let someone hold me at a concert wouldn't be for more than three years.

I told my mom about her on the phone. She referenced something in regards to me liking men, or an ex, before I said I was dating a woman. Her "I know" came deflated, as if I couldn't sense her disappointment. In the two years after Paula and I broke up, I had tried to be with dudes. Like in high school, I'd wanted to convince myself it was possible, that I could enjoy it or at least tolerate it. The closet was grueling, it suffocated me. Stewing in my shame, exhausted, lonely, and depressed, I wished to be the person so many wanted me to be. It felt like the only option.

While filming *Inception,* a friend of Leonardo DiCaprio's visited set and we had a lovely connection. Peter was warm to everyone, eyes beaming with care. When I saw Leo next, I told him I liked his friend, to which he responded that his friend liked me, too. For our first date we went to Universal Studios with Leo and his mother. Peter and I sat close on the rides, our thighs just touching.

My mom was over the moon. Prayers answered!

But my affair with Peter didn't last very long, a month, maybe two, like high school all over again.

My girlfriend and I moved in with each other too quickly. Well, sort of. She was selling her first house while I was looking to purchase my first house. The timing was absurd. Escrow closed on her place as I was to move in. So we figured—why not a temporary situation? See how it feels while she figures out her next steps? (Attempting to convince ourselves through subtext.) *That's not the same as U-Hauling.*

The congruence of our stuff, physical yes but emotional really, fueled the love, but I was yet to have names or words or tools for mine, and neither did she, at least not the correct ones from my perspective. We clogged the system and burned it to the ground.

I handled the ending horribly, ostensibly forcing her to break up with me. It needed to end, but I was incapable. Shoving my desire to leave, the sick feeling in my throat, to where I don't even know. Cringing and pulling away in bed, heartbeat rattling, my body was loud and clear. She heard it, too. I could be passionately conveying my love, my desire for a future, but also confused as the words formed on my lips. A disembodied mouth, the little plastic windup one that waddles along with its large feet. The goal was calm, and I did what I could to keep it that way.

And then I got a crush. And then I lied about said crush. And got caught in said lie. Right before the holidays at that. I made everything a complete mess. It turned into an *L Word Holiday Special*. Cut to me thinking up a stupendous idea to make a mess of the mess. I got back together with her, it stemmed from the guilt I know, whether conscious or not at the time. Easy to see now. That went on for a month. At least that time I did it, instead of manipulating her to do it. She was, rightfully so, pissed.

I loved her profoundly. I wish I'd taken greater care, that I had been further along and not placated until I snuffed the truth. Moving my finger through the flame, I made it dance before licking the tip of my index, rubbing it against my thumb and pinching, extinguishing it in an instant—that subtle hiss.

My body hoarded the unexamined emotions, sensations, wants, and needs. Easy sentences prepared in my brain, stuck. They were visible to me, written out, I heard the voice but my mouth refused to cooperate. Just the tick tick tick of the windup toy, or nothing at all.

Shingles popped out of my spine while filming *Inception* when

I was twenty-two. In a cast full of cis men, I did not understand the role I found myself in. Despite everyone being delightful to work with, I felt out of place. For the first two weeks of the film I joked I would be recast with Keira Knightley, and rightfully so. Shingles communicated the stress my body felt, what my words could not.

In our relationship I'd expected I would finally feel at home, a destination completed, quandaries resolved. She was out, and surrounded by a community of queer women, which I was now a part of. But if anything it slowly exacerbated my dysphoria. I was not settled, I still felt out of place, stirring up the dust. A pinball of projection, I internalized the chaos. It left me feeling bereft of hope.

"How can I possibly feel this way?" I bawled to my therapist. Again. "Why won't this emptiness ever go away?"

We do not realize the extent of the energy we are losing until we find where it is seeping from. Invisible until it is not. A thought just out of reach. Only now do I understand just how much I was consumed, the degree to which my brain was taken by a desperate, insatiable need to control. A watchtower enforcing my own personal isolation.

My mother recounts the incident in the car when I was fifteen differently than I do. She'd bring it up randomly, perhaps secretly wanting me to correct her, to initiate that conversation. Even changing the location from inside her VW Golf to the park.

"I remember we went for a walk in Point Pleasant Park. You were so cute when you were little, you called it Park Pleasant Park . . . Anyways, we were on a walk and you were so scared to tell me and then you did and I just got quiet and felt sad. And I think I said, 'I just don't want your life to be hard,' worried how you would be treated in this society. I feel bad I said that."

Only recently did I finally correct her, creating space for a real dialogue, a healing one. It was after my conversation with Oprah, months after sharing that I am trans. I never believed a time would come when I'd be able to have these talks with my mother. Quite frankly, I didn't think she would be open to it, and I didn't want to hurt her, to see her sad. But people can surprise you.

In the end, it was she who initiated the conversation. She was ready, and so was I. We've never been closer, and her willingness to change and grow and move through the discomfort has been powerful and inspiring. She's become my ally. She loves her son endlessly. I'm lucky to have that, to feel such profound and genuine love. What was the most beautiful and meaningful was to watch her bloom as her old narratives and doctrines faded.

Something opened up. She became less fearful. She has always been self-critical, and I grew up listening to her endlessly berate herself, always using the words "stupid" or "foolish." This has grown quieter, softer, with at least self-reflection, a readjustment, a knowing that she is worth it. As the old constructs continue to crumble, it lets my mother build something new, too. Perhaps her unconditional love for me has begun to extend to herself.

15

"RYAN"

———

At twenty-six, I assumed that most people knew I was queer, in my private life I was considerably more open and the last step would be to eventually come out publicly. But I found myself again in a deeply closeted relationship and desperately in love. My partner was more closeted than me for a change, but everything is in degrees, people meet at different points of their journey, unable to sync up the tracks. We were together for almost two years, and even some of my closest friends were not aware I was in a relationship. Her parents did not know. I was the friend that came for Christmas. Only her sister and two of her friends knew. We never touched outside, we barely went to dinner. She was in my phone under the name "Ryan."

We were staying at the Bowery Hotel in New York City. There are often paparazzi camped out across the street, waiting for celebs to pass through. When we were leaving for the day she went outside, got in a cab, turned the corner onto East Third Street, and I walked out a side door and got in. There was a period when she was working in Europe and I went to visit. She was staying in a giant corporate hotel. That sleek and modern vibe, lots of gray. We ordered room service, and when it was delivered, I literally hid in a closet. Light shone through under the door. I listened to the table roll in, the metal covers clang, and her warm voice expressing gratitude. How frighteningly casual some memories can be.

She would question queerness. Was it true, or simply a consequence of privilege, of having the space to think about it? Similar to thoughts I had when the idea of being queer felt impossible, believing as an actor that I would never be able to come out, praying to God knows what, *please make me like men*. When I think back, I questioned her sexuality, too, in a way that was harsh and unfair, prying for an answer she was not ready to give. I was angry at her, but I had all the information, I wanted to stay. Still repulsed with my entirety, truth be told, the person I was angry at was me.

Often at parties we would hardly look at each other. As if a sudden catch of the eyes would spill the queer beans.

"What, so you don't even look at each other in public?" one of my closest pals asked.

I remember one party. I wanted to go home, but she had the key and I had to get it from her. We needed to perform a stealth operation, conceal it all, sharp in the palm.

"Maybe we should both get boyfriends?" she suggested one evening as we lay in bed, to throw people off, as if that would mitigate the shame and vigilance. We were in an open relationship, so technically it was not an unreasonable question.

"I can't do that, but if you want to you should." The word "should" came out sharp, a pulled pin, it was just a matter of time now.

For an extremely closeted couple we had a lot of fun, discreet but adventurous sex. On rocks just below the Pacific Coast Highway, hidden in boulders in Joshua Tree National Park, on an airplane.

An unconscious yearning to be caught, to have no choice. Forced through the door.

We met making a film together. We would hold hands under a blanket in the back of the transpo van. Reaching instinctually. It wasn't discussed. It didn't need to be.

I remember the first time I saw her. I sat waiting in LAMILL on Silver Lake Boulevard when she walked in. She was radiant— her dress, her smile, how she pushed her hair from her face. The way she formed a thought moved me, concise, distinct, intelligent, emotional. She didn't seem afraid. Her best friend sat beside her, out of focus. We discussed books, activism, our collective consciousness, and the deep intelligence of nature. Driving south down Laurel Canyon at Sunset Boulevard, I would pass a giant photograph of her, the poster for her latest film. Her beauty is dangerous, I'd think, it'll cause a car crash.

I didn't want to come out. I wanted to be with her, we loved each other, cared deeply and had a meaningful time together. There was a lot of goodness there, healing even. We took an epic trip to Nova Scotia for her birthday. Down to Sable River, not far from my father's hometown on the south shore. We traveled north, stayed in a friend's cabin outside of Pugwash. We hiked, made food over the bonfire, swam under a waterfall. I remember napping in the late afternoon, waking up to the gloaming, her favorite time of day. She slept with my head on her chest, I soaked in the silence, her smell. *I wish I could bottle this,* I thought. I felt the quiet pain that comes with being in love, the risk of it all. We drove along the Northumberland Strait and made our way up to Cape Breton. She told people she was meditating in Maine. I said I was going to visit my folks.

We flew from Halifax to Toronto and waited for our connections in an Air Canada lounge, the space between us locked shut.

We were flying to different locations, I can't remember where. I sat drinking the free espresso while she took the book I was reading, *Sex at Dawn,* and began to write in the back sleeve, an outpouring of love, one of the most beautiful letters I have ever received. How sad we never got to flourish.

It was not a sustainable relationship, just like when I had kept people hidden. The lying, the anxiety, the disgust. People didn't "think she was queer," but they definitely assumed I was, and I don't think she could handle the shame. Ultimately, she had to do what was best for her, and unfortunately it resulted in my heart being shattered.

Not long after she ended things, one of my only friends who knew about Ryan encouraged me to get out and stop wallowing in my pain. Alia's friend Sam was having a small games night, did I actually want to go? No. But it felt important to force it, to stop with the self-pity.

"Watch Ryan be there," I joked.

"No no, she's not in that circle."

Which was true.

I sat with Alia on the cushy rug in the A-frame's living room. We sipped tequila as I attempted to lighten my tone, to lift my shoulders, muster some energy that would make me give a fuck.

About fifteen minutes later the door opened, and before I saw Ryan, I heard her, that glowing warmth in her voice. And then, his voice. He was tall and handsome, an artist with scraggly blondish hair and good style. I stood up and we locked eyes, the room melting, my knees on the brink. She stopped looking, attention returning to her date, his hand on her back. I did my best not to stare.

I beelined for the spiral staircase, gripping the metal railing. Alia followed. I stepped out onto the patio, a concrete formation built into the hill. I lit a cigarette and attempted to calm down, my heart palpitating, my hands trembling. Shortly after, they walked outside with a few others. They joined us as the rules of a game were being explained. I glanced at her, taking in how relaxed she was with him.

Unable to deal, I pretended to get sick. "Oh no, I think food poisoning," I said, hand moving to cover my mouth.

Scrambling to the washroom, I waited for time to pass, avoiding the mirror, I splashed water on my face. Back in the living room, I sat at a table, arms folded, my head resting on my forearms, looking to the side. Alia rubbed my back as Ryan's date came over with coconut water. He had no idea about our history, of course. It was a kind gesture, but I wanted to take that coconut water and throw it. Alia tried to intervene. Eventually I got up and headed outside to wait for a car. I kept the secret.

I went from a relationship where attending something like a games night together was inconceivable to watching her being touched by him, her enjoying it, existing in the way she never could with me. *I guess I should be happy for her,* I tried to convince myself. I wanted to be, to be evolved, but it was too much. It unreservedly gutted me.

Someone will break your heart but you will break one, too.

16

SPEEDO

———

I was utterly distraught when the final coed season for soccer was ending at age nine or ten, as if I were nursing a torn-up heart. My parents asked the league if I could play one more year, stalling the inevitable transition to the girls' team. To "not be separated from her friends" is how people perceived it. Yes, of course, but the seemingly undue agony wasn't just about that. The league allowed me one more season. But after that, I was with the girls.

It was humiliating when the ref would turn to me with a probing glare. My short-haired self would be setting up the ball for kickoff but then be interrupted with: "Boys can't play on this team."

"I'm a girl," I'd respond. Not precisely meaning it, but what else was there to say?

A smarmy smile would spread across his face.

Turns out, I preferred that embarrassment, the sensation that indeed I should not be on the team, an innate feeling the instant boys and girls could no longer compete as one, I'd rather that than what came next.

My chest began to grow, leading to awkward conversations about training bras, forcing me to try to find those perfectly oversize concealing T-shirts; my posture began to fold, shoulders caving in. My confidence dwindled in conjunction with my self-disgust rising. And then my period came. While I was snowboarding with my father in Wentworth, an 815-vertical-foot ski hill about an hour and a half from the city. That smell of metallic blood, a robot leaking. My dad went to the store and got pads. I fussed and fiddled until it was secure in my underwear. *I'm going to have to wear this diaper every month?* I thought. I wished I could wear a tampon due to the chafing, but no fucking way was I attempting that.

My weight redistributed in a way that I did not understand, my clothes from the Gap's boys section began to betray me. I could not detect myself. I didn't transform into me—the me I knew I was—like the other boys did. I was desperate to wake up from this bad dream, my reflection making me increasingly ill. Closing my eyes I'd find the memories, the moments of euphoria, of witnessing myself, praying I'd find that again.

An unlikely source of hope emerged. There was a kid I played soccer with until I had to be with the girls. Tim. Tim's parents had moved to Halifax from Germany around when he was born. His parents were both engineers who lived on South Street, opposite the Holy Cross Cemetery, in an older, tall red house with a storm porch welcoming you. Mr. Peltzer was a superb and exuberant soccer player, he'd give us pointers, explaining the use and importance of empty space, the movement, a small turn, one touch to find it, head up, to push it forward into the unknown.

It was sweltering out, well, my idea of sweltering at the time. Nova Scotia's summer temperatures hover around twenty to twenty-five degrees Celsius but can rise as high as thirty to thirty-two degrees with humidity. A few of us boys were at Tim's. We kicked the soccer ball around the backyard, parents would have been thrilled to know of the imminent exhaustion. Tim's dad lugged out a kiddie pool. In my memories, it is more substantial than one of those tiny ones, but maybe that's because I was the tiny one. He began to fill it up, and it struck me, I did not have my bathing suit. Out of sight, out of mind, I hated my swimsuit. I loved swim shorts. Swim trunks, my dad would call them. The words, direct, with two syllables, roused elation in my mouth. *Swim trunks.* A satisfying crunch.

"We have extra," said Tim's dad, upon sensing my concern, "you can use one of Tim's or Ben's."

My face brightened. *Tim's or Ben's?*

I followed him into the house, behind the odor of cigarette smoke. He marched up the stairs, returning to the kitchen with a small red Speedo. Holding it before me, the white drawstring dangled, as if waving.

I'll just always forget my bathing suit, I thought. I despised those fucking straps, stretching it over my body, concealing my stomach. Every sticky, wet disrobe, I'd wince as it clung, *you're stuck in here.* Boys would pinch and pick their drenched and dripping trunks from their thighs. Some glistened in the sun, their small Speedos sleek and tight, Superman's bathing suit.

"Here, you can wear this."

Exchanging hands, I was careful not to drop it, a sacred talisman, I felt acutely aware that I could not soil it in any way. Closing the bathroom door behind me, the slam unintentionally forceful, I was intoxicated by the nylon-elastane cardinal treasure. Hurriedly guiding my feet through the holes, I yanked up the Speedo. I climbed onto the toilet, or the edge of the tub, high enough so I could see in the mirror. I tightened and tied the drawstring, looking up triumphantly, grinning ear to ear.

The backyard was no different than it had been. It didn't matter that an elastic, nylon layer of skin was not hiding my chest. I was frolicking with my friends, just us kids. The only shift was in my happiness, a moment of knowing, a crisp focus, enhancing all the colors and sounds. A rush of joy.

This was only the second time I had seen a Speedo in person. The first time was when I was eight, visiting Prince Edward Island. We drove the three and a half hours, crossing the Confederation Bridge from New Brunswick to PEI, heading to my mom's pal Brenda's place. She had a farm in North Rustico, on the northern side of the island. There were a few of us there—another friend of my mother's, Sandy, came with her two children, who were close in age but a little younger than me. Their uncle, Sandy's brother Kyle, also hopped over to the island with us.

Sandy's brother was one of the only two gay people I knew (of) when I was a child. He was the kind of gay they showed on TV sometimes. The way he looked, the way he talked, the way he moved . . . a gay person. I'd find myself staring, sensing, a recognition. A fuse box tinkered with, my brain distributing microscopic sparks.

The farm was on a fifty-acre chunk of flat, fertile land. There was an old, large house with white shingles that sat proudly and a barn, behind, off to the right, sheltering the chickens that I scrambled out of bed at the first sign of light to feed. Mabel, an ancient, colossal pig, felt like a friend. I'd visit unprompted, wanting to get close, but not too close, skittish of her robustness. Conscious that reasoning with this creature was not a viable option. Opposite the barn stood a few trees, their branches protruding, bending, and curling; the perfect place. I'd remain outside for hours, building a fort, securing it from coyotes with a worn discarded hubcap that I rolled in front of the little opening. I have always loved being in nature.

During this vacation, we went to Rainbow Valley, a small amusement and water park in Cavendish. I never was that into swimming and water parks, and I speculate this had something to do with bathing suits. (I should give water parks another chance, start fresh in my swim trunks.) Waiting in line at the top of the most popular and highest slide, Kyle stood behind me in his Speedo. The wetness over his smooth skin twinkled. His firm, tanned body, the torso a dream. I tried not to look down at the tight Speedo, but I did look down at the tight Speedo. As did the teenage boys behind us.

"Faggot . . ." you could hear them whispering. The kind of mumbling made just audible enough to hear. Those fucking cowards.

I witnessed Kyle's body immediately shrink, his shoulders rounded forward, his head ever so slightly shifting downward, stretching the back of his neck. The boys, in their long swim trunks, snickered and mocked, contemptuous of queers like him, like us. I did and did not know what was going on. Kyle said nothing, his focus on me, smiling as we crept up for our turn and flung ourselves toward the earth.

It turns out I am not exactly a Speedo guy, but wearing swim trunks for the first time, chest out and with my scars visible, was indescribable. Perhaps that moment in Toronto was best captured in a photo I posted on Instagram. A smile on my face as massive as they come.

I have gone from someone who lounged around a pool in ninety-degree weather practically bundled up to standing proudly, with this body that feels my own.

"Did you bring your swimming jeans?" a friend once joked as we sat on the roof of her apartment building under the scorching LA sun.

Swimming in that backyard in Toronto, my legs kicked, my

17

CRASH

———

As an adult, whenever I was heading home, I would prep myself. I spent so much of my professional life performing that I had come to the realization that I could not also perform in my personal life. I should not have to perform, I did not have to make things okay for Linda and for my dad.

Okay, THIS time you will say something. THIS time you will stand up for yourself.

"Please don't say that."

"Why do you have to talk to me like that?"

Practicing. Performing?

But, of course, as soon as I got there I could never give my all. I'd enter the door, hellos projected up and down the stairwell, and before I had finished removing my sneakers—back pain, anxiety, gas in the gut, brick on the chest. The feeling so visceral, the glares of judgment. It hijacks your resolve, pulverizing it like the pecans for her crumble. A doll with its string pulled, auto-response on re-play, not even real. Looking back, I had been exhausting all efforts to earn her love and to keep my father content. If my dad was not defending me, clearly *I* must be the problem, and maybe, if at long last, I managed to find a solution, well, perhaps then I would feel safe. I started barely going home.

Instead, my father came to visit me in Los Angeles. I was twenty-five, living in my own place on Canton Drive—a quiet neighborhood, mostly young families and older folks. I liked it there. The house was a two-bedroom with a large backyard that had a steep incline. The scent of jasmine filled the garden—I'd planted it along the fence because I knew Ryan cherished it, the way that it suffused the air. I had a medium-size pool, shaped like a kidney bean, that glistened under the California sun. At night, the yard would light up bright purple (because a recent ex enjoyed colored lightbulbs, I kept forgetting to swap them, they eventually burned out).

The house had a decent-size living room with large windows that looked down to the street. It was sparsely furnished with a couch and two mid-century chairs that faced the white-painted brick fireplace. There was a small, sleek galley kitchen with a small half bath tucked to the left and two cozy bedrooms.

Before my father arrived, he'd told me that there were things he wanted to talk to me about this trip that had to do with my childhood. My first thought was of the animosity I'd experienced growing up from Linda, and his seeming inability to step in, or maybe he'd finally realized how his expressions of love shifted when we were alone versus with her. Dennis has a power reminiscent of Linda's but it manifests differently. He does not need those burning looks, his soft tone takes care of it, manipulating the frequency to get what he wants. Washing over, bathing you in self-doubt, it implies comfort, but it chills the skin. And you don't know why, but you go along with it.

I was too stunned on that phone call to ask what he meant, but fear and hope intermingled in my chest as I went to pick him up from the airport. The possibility of getting an apology from him, having a real conversation about it all, it felt like the time had finally come.

A day or two into his visit we sat in the parking lot of a Whole Foods after grabbing groceries. He turned to me, face filled with contemplation.

"What I wanted to talk to you about, well, I've been thinking a lot about it . . ." he began. "I feel I have carried guilt for so long and I have finally come to a place where I can let go of it."

It wasn't exactly what I'd expected but I still clung to the hope that this was the reckoning that could help us move forward.

"I've always felt so guilty for leaving your mother when you were little"—my brain twisted in confusion—"but if all that hadn't happened, I never would have been with Linda." I didn't understand why he was saying this, why he was expressing it to me. I had felt so small and powerless growing up in that house with her. He continued, "I never would have had this life with her. I never would have had the love and happiness I have. I love her so much."

I never would have had this life with her. I repeated his words to myself. This wonderful life. In that moment one thing was clear: He didn't see it at all. He didn't see me at all.

My lungs stopped working, chest on fire but still, the car a trap. The last time I was home I'd finally been able to share some of my experience, of my pain and the impact of growing up in that house. Here, again, it seemed my feelings were pushed aside, erased, an emotional punch to the gut.

I stared ahead, frozen and silent, my brain unable to follow the rest of the conversation. It wasn't that I was not speaking, it was that I couldn't speak, a sensation that has escorted me throughout my life, an imperceptible muzzle, hushing without notice. My level of discomposure has caused issues at work. The mirror, my face, the tight clothes, I did want to die, but I wasn't going to do it, not consciously at least. The convenient and closest alternative was to shut it all down, trigger an outage. When these outages happen, I often lose myself to memory—stress piling on stress.

My mind slipped to another moment.

"Can you speak up?!"

I was at a fancy, prestigious photo shoot, with a famous, acclaimed photographer, I sat in a director's chair getting my hair and makeup done. I'd arrived at the most elaborate shoot I'd been to at the time. There was music pumping, flashes were tested in the periphery of my vision, a myriad of people, the hippest of the hip. It was like in the movies.

Already quiet and shy, I walked in and was introduced to the stylist. There was no fitting, because there was only a single option, and I had to wear it. A blue dress that was too tight and did not fully zip up the back squeezed the last morsel of confidence out of me, and then it happened, words narrowly made it out of my mouth. An indiscernible mumble.

The world-renowned photographer had pulled a matching chair up to introduce herself. The makeup artist paused so she could say hello, asking me the questions you ask when you first meet, but I couldn't supply the answers. Something else took control, my body stiff, not responding. Her irritation with me grew visible, it began with a look that could be interpreted as confusion but promptly turned to malice.

"Do you even talk?" she snapped sharply.

As the sentence emerged, she raised her leg, a slight lean backward. She pulled her knee up and back toward her. With force, she kicked the side of my chair. The base of her boot striking the wooden frame. Hard. My heart skipped. It was all so quick. *What the fuck just happened?*

Stunned, I sank lower. As she walked off I did what I could to prevent tears from ruining the makeup. *You can't have runny eyeliner, for goodness' sake.* I can't recall whether her kick elicited a reply from me. All I know is that they completed their polishing, made my hair sleek and wavy, and, with costume donned, I had my picture taken.

We pulled into my driveway. Now panic swept through me, but I couldn't explain why, not even to myself. Looking back, I now know that even the thought of having to contradict his version of the truth sent me on a tailspin. Anxiety in the bones.

After unpacking groceries, I grabbed my cell phone, my wallet, and my sunglasses, saying I had to head to my therapy appointment, regretting that I had shared the appointment time with him. There was a masked tension, the exaggerated nice, actors in a play, the fireplace simply a prop, none of it real.

"It's not for two hours."

"I know, just so much traffic to get over the hill this time of day and I want to grab a coffee."

Driving down Laurel toward Ventura Boulevard, my body shook. My right leg inadvertently jounced, a subtle rattling in my kneecap. Concentrating, I willed my foot to calm. Looking out the windshield, my focus blurry, red light, green light, a tiny bit of gas, I took a left onto Moorpark. Three shots of espresso on ice, topped with a splash of soy milk, rested in my Mini's cup holder. Up to Ventura, I would take Coldwater Canyon to go from the Valley to my therapist's old office in Beverly Hills on Wilshire Boulevard. I'd be early, I'd enjoy my coffee in the car.

My trembling getting worse, I turned on NPR, looking for a

soothing voice to drown out my loud thoughts. Taking an occasional sip, the caffeine obviously not aiding my efforts to ease my angst. Sweating but cold, stomach churning, shit demanding out. Like a jump scare, but I stayed in the air. I tried to focus, eyes on the road.

Stopped now at a red, I went to change lanes to pull around the vehicle in front of me. A simple maneuver, one I'd done tons of times in LA traffic. I hit the car's right rear light, smashing the front left of my car and thankfully doing far less harm to theirs. Following the black sedan into a parking lot off Ventura, I was nauseated with guilt. I'd never had an instance like this as a driver before. The woman was shaken, I apologized profusely.

"Were you texting or something?!" she inquired angrily, understandably so.

"No, I wasn't, I don't know why I did that. I'm so terribly sorry."

We exchanged information, took photos. Insurance did their thing, unmistakably my fault, no doubt there.

I got back in the car, looked at the time. I phoned my therapist, shame showering me, utterly distraught.

"Ellen, these things happen, fender benders happen every day. I've done it."

Her words satiated me, helping settle my stomach. Stabilizing, I'd still be able to make it for a decent chunk.

Sitting on my therapist's couch, I was curled over, head in hands, aching with guilt. She worked to talk me down, but it wouldn't penetrate, I could not let it in. Somehow, the conversation led to my father.

"Do you want to have your father come in with you while he's here?"

I barely let her complete the sentence. A quiet snap.

"What? No." It came out sharp, but with a soft laugh of disbelief. An unexpected reaction, the kind I store away for my work.

She asked why. I didn't have an answer really, other than absolutely not.

The thought of confronting him, setting any boundary at all, made me feel like I was going to shit blood.

Having to deal with the car situation at least allowed for a proper distraction when I returned home. Phone calls, a drive to the dealership for repair. My dad is very much a car guy. My uncle is a mechanic, as well as two cousins. So he went into his zone, and I ceded control to him, which let me stay in mine.

As the day went on, I repeated different versions of sentences over and over in my head, building my strength, or stalling, I'm not sure. But I couldn't do it. The words just couldn't come out. Feelings locked shut, close, but always shoved back.

You blur the boundaries enough, you get lost in between. It was that moment I felt I would never hear what I yearned for, an understanding, or at least an explanation. Something. It would take me years to finally speak.

18

INTUITION

———

When I was twelve, I was sitting on the toilet and I *knew*. I had been reminded by my parents that day that this "acting thing" would not be my future.

"This won't be forever, I don't want you to get your hopes up," they would say.

Understandably, our environment was far removed from film-making, Hollywood more a myth than a place. My parents did not doubt me in a mean way, but a realistic one, not wanting me to get ahead of myself or get too excited. It would be a fun experience now, but I needed to keep up my grades and play soccer. Acting wouldn't be a career.

But I *knew*. The clarity of that moment is something I will never forget. I sat an inordinate amount of time on the loo, staring at nothing but everything. I split open, an inexplicable feeling. Of all actors, Julia Roberts popped up, which is a delightful coincidence, considering I did the revamp of *Flatliners*.

Someone probably said that to Julia Roberts, that it would never happen. Unrealistic, too hard, not possible. But it was and it is. I know it is going to happen, I can see it. I can feel it.

I never told anyone, it was my little secret. I sensed it deep within, and I never doubted from that point on that I would stick with it. Becoming accustomed to the rejection, I was not fazed by it. *Some parts I will get and other actors are disappointed. Some parts I will not get and then it's my turn to be disappointed.* It doesn't mean you aren't upset, heartbroken even, it just means you roll with it. Perhaps I just got it out of my system early. Like a lot of things, you get used to it.

I would run lines with my best friend at the time. We had known each other since primary, but it was when we were paired together for a science fair project as preteens that we first spent time alone. Jack and I quickly became inseparable.

He would read scenes with me, ensuring that I had memorized everything I needed to. My family did not have a video camera, and he would go to a studio downtown with me to make self-tapes when the auditions were not in person. The casting directors would fax me scenes, called sides, that I would record on VHS and then mail back to them; eventually the tapes were replaced with CDs.

Jack and I were weird kids together. We invented a game called tree bouncing where we sat on a circular piece of wood while holding on to a long piece of rope that dangled from the massive tree in Jack's yard and launch ourselves off the trunk. The challenge was to spin as much as we could before the bottoms of our feet reconnected with the oak, often leaving one of us slamming our back or side into the hard bark. No pain, no gain. We even had our own political party, the Pigeon Party—our manifesto was hard to pin down, but we'd wander the streets advocating for pigeon rights, interviewing any stray birds we found. They typically waddled away from our requests.

Jack was teased pretty severely. He was often hyper, very hyper, which definitely annoyed some people. One kid would shove Jack against the lockers and attempt to stuff him in, harassing him virtually every day. The same kid forced me into a garbage bin once. Classmates were vicious, stirring him up and making his temper explode. This only made them pick on him harder. I wanted to be there for him. He was there for me, too. We needed each other.

Jack's father died when he was three and his stepfather was not the warmest man. And perhaps I am projecting, but his stepdad was noticeably kinder to his biological son. It filled me with fury, but what could I do? Jack was just a kid, isolated in grief, with no place to put it.

"You would be cool if you did not hang out with Jack," a different friend said to me while we played tennis near his house on Tower Road. We'd been best friends in elementary school, but since junior high our friendship was slipping—he had entered the popular group, and I was not into the "cool stuff." I was into making up bizarre games with Jack and filming myself reading random scripts that came out of the fax machine. I wanted to be around someone who didn't put up a front. As much as was possible for me at the time, I was myself with Jack. I suppose my aversion to "coolness" and "popularity" related to the degree to which I was already masking myself, fully aware of it or not, and popularity is the ultimate mask. A mold too tight. I felt compressed enough.

But it was Jack who helped me land my first lead in a film when I was fourteen. I got the part based off a self-tape we made downtown. The sides sprawled out on the floor, Jack making me laugh as he played the different parts. Just us. I could disappear, leave the body for a moment, paradoxically allowing me to connect to my body more. This would happen when I went away to film. The clothes and hair were not always fun, but the joy I got to feel while acting, that permission to leave, I could breathe. I have so much to thank Jack for.

The film was called *I Downloaded a Ghost* and it was about a teenager who . . . you guessed it, downloads a ghost off the internet. Carlos Alazraqui, now one of the stars of *Reno 911!*, was the ghost. He was incredible at impressions. I would ask him to do them over and over, particularly Homer Simpson. He was hilarious and nice and patient with me; it isn't always easy working with kids.

It filmed in Saskatoon, Saskatchewan, the farthest I'd ever been from home. The woman who played the bully, who was not a teenager but in her early twenties playing a teen, was beautiful and sincere and treated me kindly. My crush on her overwhelmed me, a vibration, the way light circled her. When I was back at school in Halifax, I'd fantasize about her waltzing into the classroom, I really believed she might. How self-involved was I? I did and did not fully understand that I was crushing. All I knew was I could not stop thinking about her, I *missed* her. Could she tell I had a crush? I'm not sure.

I ached when projects ended, not yet accustomed to the intense on-set bond being abruptly broken. Working fueled me—it forced me to be in the present, forced me to feel. Being away from school, as much as I was during those years, you would think my grades suffered, but they didn't. The opportunity to learn one-on-one with a tutor, with all the implied focus and care, meant that my lack of confidence in the classroom did not extend to a trailer or an office in the soundstage with school books scattered about. We could just do the work.

After *I Downloaded a Ghost,* jobs kept coming, a noticeable build. *Something is happening, this could happen,* I thought. I wanted a space that would allow for some autonomy, that reflected reality in a way that school did not. I was addicted to the fresh start I got on every film set. Enthralled by possibility, I poured my whole self into that world—I was in a place where being a weird kid was good. I didn't want to look back.

I was cast as the lead in a film called *Ghost Cat,* a family film whose premise is, again, what you may expect from the title. As Rotten Tomatoes aptly puts it: *A spectral feline causes mischief after a man (Michael Ontkean) and his teenage daughter move into an old house.* It was only my second time being the lead in a film, coincidentally both with the word "ghost" in the title.

It was on this set that I met Mark. I had just turned sixteen and he was fourteen and shorter than me at the time. Mark was the voice of the beloved aardvark Arthur for years, in what had been one of my favorite TV shows growing up, between that and having just seen his sensational performance in *The Interrogation of Michael Crowe,* I was thrilled to meet him. My character was the new kid in town, and he played the kind young neighbor I befriended.

The director, Don McBrearty, was wonderful to work with. He was kind and gave good notes. The story was in many ways about a girl dealing with profound grief and change, disconnected from her new surroundings and herself. I caught myself in the reflection of a framed photograph before action, the way my long hair shaped my face, my forehead gleaming. *Who is that?* A wave of nausea. ACTION. Disappear.

It was a couple months later in Montreal, where I was making my next project, a Lifetime movie called *Going for Broke* starring Delta Burke, that Mark and I properly became close. Where something clicked and eternally remains. We had stayed in touch and planned to get together in the city, he was there working on a film, too, but we hadn't spoken yet.

I was flipping through a chord book and clumsily strumming my Art & Lutherie, an acoustic guitar that happened to be made in Quebec. Playing simple songs, I quietly sang. Bob Dylan, Cat Stevens, the Beatles, even some of my own songs, when the hotel phone rang.

"Hello?" I said.

"Hi!" It was Mark.

He'd been out walking, and as he passed the hotel he just knew, *Ellen is staying there.* The automatic doors moved to the side as he made his way to the front desk and asked confidently, "Can I be connected to Ellen Page's room, please." And out of the many, many hotels in downtown Montreal, there I was. Mark describes it as some strange, strong intuition, he felt sure.

This was the first time Mark and I spent time together alone. With no other castmate or tutor or parent present, he opened up in a new way, a sadness slipped out. Always so sweet, thoughtful, patient, perfect really, he needed a break from that, he needed someone to say, "How are you doing?" And mean it. He was struggling. Isolated from peers. At home, at school, at work, feeling detached and empty and unclear why. Immense pressure to act, with little yield of pleasure. There was a crack and I watched it grow in front of me, a good one, necessary, the green forcing its way through the concrete.

Periodically he'd apologize for sharing so much, shame himself for his feelings. I wanted him to have space to express himself unfiltered, encouraging Mark to let go, to not censor with me or for me. I could sense the tension and wished he could relax, for the strained forehead to release.

Our time together in Montreal is marked for me by music. We listened to Radiohead endlessly, and Mark, a much better guitarist than me, helped with my rudimentary cover of "Fake Plastic

Trees." But this time was marked not just by Thom Yorke's distinctive voice, but also by our deep level of connection, of honesty and recognition—these moments, shared by two kids, led to our lifelong friendship.

Mark is how I first learned about Interact, the academic program in Toronto that I would end up attending a year later. There, I suppose I played a similar role, creating a space where Mark could be fully himself and, in return, as much as possible, so could I. He'd been much more sheltered than me, with rather overprotective parents. He was always around them, at school, or at work. You see this with a lot of child actors, isolated but never alone.

Other than when I was a little kid with my mom, I'd barely used the subway in Toronto. At fifteen, I first navigated the TTC solo when traveling downtown from my aunt's place in Etobicoke, where we visited that summer. Listening to Coldplay's *Parachutes* on my yellow Sony portable CD player, I'd read through sides for whatever auditions I had on the docket that day. Between that and only a month of living in Toronto, I already knew my way around the city better than Mark. I think his parents resented me for helping orchestrate badly needed independence, room for Mark to decide what he actually wanted and yearned for.

Our relationship has been about helping each other find the truth, to push through our fears, our egos, and meaningless expectations. We protected that honesty, a safe space to land, a person who will see you, even if you try to hide it. In many ways, the deep knowing I experienced with Mark mirrored what I'd left behind with Jack.

Jack and I drifted apart when I switched schools. Our interests shifted, and I was away for long periods to film. My new friends inspired me in many ways, made me bolder, more aware, my ignorance on display. I protested for the first time in grade ten, marching against the Iraq War. We shared books by the likes of Naomi Klein and Arundhati Roy. A sense of self was forming, deep in there, I could feel it brewing. And as my interests expanded, so did my taste in film. And this is where acting took a turn. The roles and stories were more mature, fraught emotions to be pushed and pulled and mined. I wanted more, to plunge. So I left Halifax after grade ten for Toronto. Figured I'd give it a shot. I think Jack felt abandoned. I felt it, too, even as the person leaving. It was one of the most profound friendships of my life.

When we were twenty-two or so Jack and I reunited for the first time in years. There had been some communication. Our birthdays are two days apart, I'm the twenty-first of February, and he's the twenty-third, so we'd text around then, a brief exchange, a quick catch-up. I met him at his apartment on South Park Street, just a couple buildings down from the YMCA where I had attended preschool. Jack's condo was high up, with a balcony overlooking the Public Gardens across the street. He'd built a successful life, and he seemed happy in it. We were lucky to catch each other, as both of us traveled frequently. It was nice to talk, it had been so long, we were adults now.

19

OLD NAVY

———

The OLD NAVY sign seduced my mother like a moth to a dwindling gas lantern. She fluttered with the minute strength that remained, the outcome she had been aiming for, mere yards away. Somewhere on the outskirts of Richmond, Virginia, I would walk through that chain store door, knackered and depleted by the endless judgment, but determined to emerge "a girl" for her.

My mother's life was not easy. A single mom, a working parent, and someone who had been familiar with loss from an early age. She was born in 1954 in Saint John, New Brunswick, to Gladys Jean and Gordon Philpotts, an Anglican minister. They moved frequently during my mom's childhood, living in Saint John then Toronto then Halifax. My aunts always spoke of their parents fondly, sorrow still present in their voices and the silences. Their dad died suddenly when my mother was sixteen, a heart attack. His funeral was held in St. Paul's, the oldest Protestant church in Canada. It overflowed with people, standing in the back, out the door, love and reverence from all those who'd been moved by him. My mom tells me he made his sermons joyful, youthful. Standing at the altar when he was the minister at St. Paul's, he would reference Beatles lyrics, interweaving them with the words and lessons of Jesus.

My grandmother, despite dealing with such profound grief, stayed strong for her children in the wake of her husband's death. She had no choice really, being the sole parent of four kids still at home. She kept her pain hidden from those around her. Two years after my grandpa's passing, my grandmother felt a lump in her breast and then more lumps. She made the choice to not tell her doctor, survival was highly unlikely then, she did not want to pursue treatment. My grandmother told no one, including her children. She hid it, covering what may have been a fungating breast tumor with talcum powder, Kleenex, and perfume as the cancer took over. I can imagine she did not want her children to witness that, still so fresh with grief.

My grandmother died when my mother was away studying. My mom had set off for France to study abroad as part of her degree. She longed to be a French teacher, she relished the language, the flow, the adventure of learning a familiar but new landscape. In Paris, she studied the dialect, immersed in a new culture. There is a photo of her standing in front of a fountain alone, cobblestones under her feet. The city of romance, where my father would propose to her a few years later. A long light-brown coat, chic and elegant, drops to the top of her shins. A soft smile lights up her face, her short, neat hair highlighting her cheekbones. French new wave, strikingly beautiful.

My mom did not get to attend her mother's funeral. It was the 1970s, you couldn't just pick up the phone and call. You could not send a fax. Her family tried everything, through the school, even calling bars that they learned were popular with students, but they could not track her down. Walking in town one day, my mom spotted a post office and sensed she should call home. Her brother-in-law, who lived in New Jersey, answered.

"Oh, hi, John! What are you doing there?" she asked.

Not sure what to say, he handed the phone to my aunt Beth, who also wasn't sure what to say and handed the phone to my aunt Heather, who delivered the news to my mother. Gladys Jean Philpotts had died and the funeral had already taken place.

A complete shock, unbearable pain, a nightmare. My mom's friends got her back to the dorm.

"Should we call your sisters? Figure out how to get you home?" they asked.

My mom made the decision to stay in France and finish her studies. It is what her mom would have wanted, she knew that to her core.

My heart shatters when I think of my mom's eventual flight home, hell in the clouds, asthmatic in the smoke-filled plane. Solitary and forlorn. An unimaginable ache. The thump of the wheels landing, returning to the earth, the reality you are left with.

At twenty, my mother no longer had parents.

Now home from France, she embarked on another year at Mount Saint Vincent University in Halifax. Her two younger sisters moved from Nova Scotia to New Jersey to live with my aunt Heather, the oldest, who had married an American engineer and relocated to Vineland. Heather had an effervescence and a deeply nurturing quality, perhaps sprouting from this difficult period, offering it amid her own state of grief. Dragging it out of herself. It couldn't have been easy. I can't imagine the depths of my mother's sadness when many years later Aunt Heather was diagnosed with colon cancer and also passed away.

Aunt Heather moved to Virginia, and my mom and I would go

down to see her. Those trips were special, memories where my mom was vibrant and joyful. I would climb up on Aunt Heather's bed and snuggle up by her side to watch her favorite shows, all British comedies. When my mom watched with us, she would snort while laughing, making me howl louder. It was nice. I liked seeing them happy together, those wide grins.

Aunt Heather's house was just outside of Richmond. At Aunt Heather's, with my cousins, we played outdoors and swam in a nearby lake. Once we went to the dump and found an old, battered go-kart that worked for about fifteen minutes, a quarter of an hour that I will never forget. After it broke down, we found a discarded tetherball set that seemed just fine. An adult assembled it for us, securing it to the ground, and we ended the evening with s'mores by the fire.

I would be outside for hours, sitting in the dirt and watching the ants crawl over my palm, circling it, tiny legs scrambling. I wanted to be like Mowgli, how he ate ants in the jungle. Curving around the side of my hand they reached my knuckles, recalibrating, they headed toward my wrist, scurrying around my watch. And as they did I licked them up one by one. My cousin ran off and tattled on me to my mother. Martha Philpotts marched over and furiously stuck her fingers in my mouth, digging around to remove the dead or wriggling insects. I remember she pulled out her index finger and it had streaks of black and blood. Gross, but they probably had a much higher nutrition content than the Kraft cheese slices in my aunt's fridge.

When puberty hit, around the time of my final visit, Virginia felt different. Cousins from Aunt Heather's extended family were over as well. We rarely saw each other, my mom and I couldn't go to Richmond often, but Aunt Heather's place was always a hub of activity and visitors, even in her last year.

"Where'd you get your T-shirt?" my older cousin snarled. The vibration cracking the fissure that had started when they realized I was not like them. It was thinly striped, one of my most worn. It had subtle color shifts, earth tones. Green basketball shorts, dark and shiny, topped my legs. Sporty white socks stretched proudly out of my Adidas. A chunky Casio watch circled my wrist.

Turned out, she was not interested in where I got the shirt but interested in telling me she hated it and that I dressed weirdly. Her American Eagle and Old Navy tank tops, hoodies, and jeans had made her a carbon copy of the girls who had grown to despise me. A look my way causing their faces to crinkle.

That same state of displacement, of detachment, had followed me the two thousand kilometers to Virginia.

"Do you even have a mall in Canada?" she asked.

Tongue-tied, I thought of the go-kart. The lake and how warm it was. The angry ducks. The cold Pepsis on the beach. The frozen chocolate bars that blew my mind.

Why did I think here would be different? Why would this fourteen-year-old "tomboy" fit in here?

My cousin had her sweet sixteen while we were in Virginia. She had a party planned at her mom's house, a short drive's distance. I was invited. She was popular and looked the part, so I knew the party was going to be the coolest I had ever attended. I did not want to be ridiculed, and I wanted gone with the little boy. I wanted to make my mother happy.

"Mom, will you take me to Old Navy to get girl clothes?" I asked. Typically there was no disposable income for a random wardrobe request, but this was different. This was a dream come true for Martha. There was a verve in her voice that soothed my ears, as if she'd been replenished. I liked seeing her smile.

"Oh yes, Ellen, of course!" She beamed.

Her enthusiasm spread like bong smoke getting you second-hand high. We sped down the Virginia highway, the humidity hit like a brick, always an adjustment, generating that sticky layer of moisture on your skin. We pulled into an industrial park that looked identical to the one on the outskirts of Halifax. The swaths of parking spots, patiently waiting for the shoppers, perfectly mapped out, a little incomplete rectangle for everyone. Gargantuan stores with names I knew lined the sea of painted cement. GAP, AMERICAN EAGLE, OLD NAVY. Signs stuffed in the windows advertised sales and fresh looks, pop tunes filtered out of the automatic doors, a siren song.

As my mom parked and approached, she was more or less dancing, her body, wriggling like the ants with delight, seventh heaven discovered in a parking lot. Old Navy didn't exist in the industrial park in Halifax yet, plus they had the best deals. The doors parted as she pranced in, ready to pounce. Here was her chance.

I remember surrendering as we walked through the Girl section, the pinks and baby blues, the sparkles, the tank tops, the crop tops, the low-rise jeans, all of it morphed together, the pop frequency tapping into the brain. Sentences inspired by the birth of "Girl Power" garnished the graphic tees.

My mom pulled articles of clothing off the rack, speaking a kilometer a minute. Staring at the Boy section across the room, I nodded mindlessly. Was there something else I was supposed to do?

Changing into the tight clothes, I turned and stared at the dressing room mirror. I saw someone new, or someone maybe I'd met before, I was nervous to say "nice to meet you." They stood looking right at me, directly in my eyes. She scanned my body up and down as I did hers. The light-blue tank with a small pattern of lace. The skinny jeans framed her ass, pushing it out for the world to see. Slipping into the shirt with OLD NAVY embroidered on the front, it curved into my chest, clinging to the lingering sweat.

There I was, framed like a poster, a mannequin in the window. I had value now. I needed to pull up my bootstraps, grow up, stop being difficult and selfish. Be a young lady, and make my mom proud.

Martha's high continued as we drove back to my aunt's. I watched her face. Every glance at the bags at my feet another hit, a big inhale with a smooth exhale. Now she could relax, it wasn't just a dream. The spinning top fell. The same music from Old Navy followed me through the radio, the summer hits on repeat, *Gitchie, gitchie, ya-ya, da-da (da-da-da) Gitchie, gitchie, ya-ya, here (ooh, yeah, yeah).*

The party began calmly enough, then snowballed into the kind of party I'd seen in movies starring Jennifer Love Hewitt. They were not supposed to be drinking, but shockingly, alcohol was everywhere. I had yet to *really* try liquor, other than sips of a parent's beer here and there and the champagne cocktail I was allowed on New Year's Eve that made me frolic about the house until I fell into a peaceful slumber. My days of high school parties had not quite arrived, but they would soon, where drinking was a sport as much as the soccer we played.

A friend of my cousin's sat down next to me, drunk, and started asking me about Canada.

"Do you live in an igloo?" he questioned sincerely.

I explained that I did not live in an igloo. He continued to tell me how much Canada sucks.

Parents were at home, just respectfully tucked away. Guests continued to waltz in. The music volume had incrementally risen, making it a struggle to hear much. As the pullulating house vibrated with hip-hop bass, I looked down at my chest, the tiny bumps. My new wardrobe was not the magic fix I'd hoped it would be. The layers were lighter but the discomfort heavier.

Maybe if I keep trying, keep practicing, it'll come. Yeah, it just takes effort, a choice.

But when I returned to Halifax and walked through the school doors, voilà, success. *Tout de suite,* the hot girls praised my clothes. My Old Navy jeans clung to my legs, my tank top revealed more skin than I had shown before at school, apart from in the girls' changing room.

"That shirt is so cool."

I knew it would do the trick, I thought proudly. I could win at this game.

"You have a nice ass," Katie said as she rounded a corner. She looked back over her shoulder, a covert smile, her hair following. I wanted her to like *his* ass.

"Now you just have to change the music you listen to," suggested a friend on my soccer team in the car on the way to a game, her hair tied back in a tight ponytail. I liked Radiohead and Björk, "weird music." I'd throw away myself, but not my songs.

The reaction to the girl I met in the mirror in an Old Navy in an industrial park on the outskirts of Richmond, Virginia, was what I'd wished for, but my response to that attention was not. It only heightened the sting, stretching and contaminating the wound, more of its grotesqueness on display.

Still, I couldn't shake my mother's glow, her happiness, the feeling that all was right with the world after so much pain. I wanted to give her that, but my new look began to fade. A graph with dueling lines.

20

JUST LEAN IN

Nikki wasn't like the other kids. She was authentic, she was gentle, she was bold. Her smile, *that smile,* welcomed you in. Her red hair, thick and wavy, framed her face. I'd turn my body to look back, my stomach rattling, pop rocks crackling off. My vocal cords quivering, struggling to form words, I'd plummet into her green eyes and afterward regret whatever I had said. It was tenth grade, and I was in love.

She sat behind me in English class. I recognized her from playing basketball in junior high school. She went to Cunard Junior High, the same school my siblings had gone to. Scott and Ashley's dad was a teacher at Cunard. Nikki had really liked him.

I remembered her from the court because I could not stop looking at her—a force, an electromagnetic pull. It baffled me the way some girls would affect me. All humans emit radiation, frequency. Was it the vibration? The invisible reaching?

A *Scientific American* article by Tam Hunt explains:

> An interesting phenomenon occurs when different vibrating things/processes come into proximity: they will

often start, after a little time, to vibrate together at the same frequency. They "sync up," sometimes in ways that can seem mysterious.

"You asked me to stop being so pushy guarding you. Ha ha," Nikki shared with her charming grin.

My heart bounced, it was not just me, that moment, that game. It wasn't mine alone, she remembered me, too.

From that point on I always beelined for a desk close to hers. I searched for excuses to look. She wore socks and Birkenstocks, cozy sweaters, and had the best fucking laugh, utterly infectious. Her sense of humor got me.

"Sweater vests, solving the age-old problem, hot arms, cold chest," she said, completely deadpan, in reference to her puffy vest.

I cackled noisily. An uncontrollable, energetic swell merged with a burst of ebullience, I was about to combust. *What the fuck was happening to me?*

Ugh, I was too hyper. She probably thinks I'm annoying. Be more chill next time. Be. More. Chill.

I wanted to know her better, I wanted to move the desks aside. I was transfixed, I was spellbound.

Despite my feelings, I pursued boys. There was a cute guy who had dirty blond hair and an interesting face with piercing eyes and a strong jaw. I did not necessarily enjoy kissing him, but I loved the adventure of it, the potential, *maybe I can like a boy?* We did not spend much time together in junior high, but the intimidation of this new frontier found us leaning on each other. Or perhaps he just wanted his dick sucked.

We'd hook up secretly in hidden corners around school. We would roll around together in the girls' soccer room, where my teammates and I would prepare for practice. It reeked of stinky shin pads and scrimmage uniforms that needed a wash, a cloak of stale sweat. The space was chaotic, with one of those very large, very thick blue crash mats off to the side.

We lay on the cushy surface, making out, touching, dry humping.

He and I shared French class together. Despite my mother being bilingual, it was always my worst subject. She didn't speak French with me as a child, which I mildly resent, and I struggled, languages never a strong suit. So, it was a delight to have a reason to escape, especially when a covert operation was taking place. He'd sit behind me and pass me a note.

Meet me at the boys' bathroom

Raising his hand, the teacher nodded.

"Est-ce que je peux aller aux toilettes?"

"Oui."

My lover rose and left the room. I let some time pass and then stuck my arm up.

"Est-ce que je peux aller aux toilettes?"

"Oui."

I left the room and took a right down the deserted hallway. He stood outside *les toilettes* with an endearing confidence that couldn't quite conceal his nerves. The bathroom was vacant, soundless. We crept in, whispering, and sped into a stall, looking at each other with mischievous smirks. Lips smacking, he put this hand on my breasts, my nipples grew hard. Fussing with his pants, he zipped open the fly, and pulled his cock out, perky and firm. He spit on his hand to moisten his dick, stroking it until my hand replaced his.

"Will you suck it?" he asked, his eyes begging for it.

I got on my knees. Holding his penis, I lined it up with my mouth, opening wide, inviting it in.

Our extracurricular activities were typically focused on his pleasure.

A staggered return to class, him first, me second.

I wanted to be in Nikki's friend circle, but I wasn't, not quite yet.

My French class escapades started to taper off. The thrill faded, sensation not outweighing risk. And you can't be going to the bathroom the same time every class or *le professeur* will catch on. Dry humping in the soccer room also lost its appeal—I had grown bored and numb. *Why couldn't I feel more?* I wondered at the time. The salivating that surrounded me, the urges, the boys, the girls . . . *were others pretending, too?*

Nikki and I were becoming more and more comfortable with each other. Transitioning from acquaintances to companions, an equal desire for closeness. My crush deepened. If she sat close, I'd wonder, *was that on purpose?* When she laughed and squeezed my upper arm, I'd think, *maybe I should laugh and touch her back?* I would giggle and quickly touch her shoulder. It felt like a new form of communication, disguised Morse code. I could not say the words outright, so my body searched for a way to transcribe them.

On Nikki's eighteenth birthday, I biked across the city, heart thundering, to bring her a card. The front had an illustration of two women communicating something suggestive, lesbian innuendo. I wish I could remember what it was. I purchased it at Biscuit General Store downtown, one of the first, if not the first, hipstery clothing spots in the city. We loved that place.

Could I say what my intention was? I don't know. It all felt mindless, it was just happening. When I bought the card, when I wrote in the card, when I sped across the city to deliver it to her with a gift. I had texted her on my thick Nokia cell phone to let her know I was on the way. Pumping my thighs, propelling forward, that vibration again. I couldn't get there fast enough.

I tracked her down and handed it to her. She held the white envelope with two hands, staring down. Sweat dripped between the middle of my breasts. Nikki opened it, laughed at the card, and then I handed her *Siddhartha* by Hermann Hesse, one of my favorite books.

She hugged me, thanked me for the gift, and went back to her day. The instant I left I was mortified. A feeling reminiscent of when at sixteen I fell in love with a woman in her thirties I'd met on a film. I made her a mix CD and dropped it in the lobby of the Drake—a chic hotel in Toronto. After the fifteen-minute walk, when I returned to the silence of my small yellow room, I turned to pieces. *What the fuck did I just do?* I flew downstairs, raced the laces, and took off. Raining now, I sprinted, fraught with humiliation. *No no no no.* Out of breath I pushed on. *Okay, run in, get the CD back and no one will be the wiser.*

I waited impatiently behind someone checking in. *Come on, come on.*

"Hi, I just dropped something off for someone, but I need to get it back . . ."

"Oh, she actually just got back and took it up with her," a clerk with a cool haircut at the desk responded.

She was probably listening to "Anthems for a Seventeen-Year-Old Girl" right now, finding it adorable that I had a crush. I may as well have shat blood. My heart itself passing through, straight into the toilet.

"Thank you for the music, I really like it," she said the next time

I saw her. Staring down with an endearing smile, an invisible pat on the head, as if to say—*how cute.*

I hoped, without much faith, that this time would be different.

Nikki and I skirted around our chemistry, hovering and ducking. We'd hang out constantly, it felt romantic at times. I was nearly certain it was not just me, but maybe it was, maybe I was the only queer.

I remember sitting together in her mother's beige Toyota Camry at Dingle Park, not wanting to drive home just yet. The sun was setting, just about to disappear for the night. We sat in the quiet, staring out at the Arm. I thought we might kiss. Eventually, the sun winked from the tip of the horizon, saying its final goodbyes. I smiled at her, she smiled back. I remember how beautiful she looked. I could hear my heart and hoped she couldn't also. A few beats went by and we both exhaled, circumventing once more, we turned our heads to face forward. We waited in the car until the night took hold.

Moments like these hid in our friendship, tucked away, unnamed. Another time we were huddled in a small tree house in her backyard. The classic kind, just wood, a small trapdoor. Nikki's dad had made it for her. He had died when she was eight.

We smoked a joint, getting lost in conversation as the crickets joined in. The house was dark, except for the living room, the light radiated out. Inside, her mother watched television, distracted by the flickering glow. Our faces were close, Nikki looked right at me and I looked right back. Time stopped, the corners of our mouths offering the tiniest beginnings of a grin. We did not move.

Lean in, I thought. *You just need to* lean in.

I didn't, neither did she, and the moment passed. We climbed down from the tree.

So many times where all I had to do was lean in, lean in to her and to myself, but I couldn't. And eventually, I lost my chance. One evening, we lay on her bed talking. Her arm was around me, allowing me to nestle into her, the closest we'd ever been. I glanced up, a new angle. Her neck stretched as she looked to the ceiling, her chin pointed proudly. Nikki's eyes moved downward, her head following behind, a new angle for her, too. Her lips, pink and full. I wanted them on my mouth.

"Nikki?" The door opened.

Immediately disconnecting, we created space in between. This was useless, we had already been caught.

Slowly, we began to drift apart.

The lead of the school musical asked Nikki to prom shortly after. He was tall, handsome, popular, friends with everyone, the kind of person who can move their way in and out of various groups and cliques without having to mutate. Talented, smart, funny . . . desirable.

Nikki said yes. The moment I found out, I felt my heart split. Earlier in the year she and I made casual remarks about going together, a hidden moment that evaporated like the rest. Yet some small part of me believed we would. I wanted to yell, to say go with me, to say I love you, but nothing came out. The image of someone else's lips on hers stirred a new sensation. Pumped by the heart, jealousy revealed itself, cycling through my body.

Nikki and I did not completely lose touch. Years later, she told me she had felt the same.

I resent that we were cheated out of our love, that beautiful surge in the heart stolen from us. I am furious at the seeds planted without our consent, the voices and the actions that made our roads to the truth unnecessarily brutal.

She still has the copy of *Siddhartha* I gave her, with the inscription inside:

NIKKI—

I am not always great with words in regards to expressing feelings and sharing my thoughts. As you turn 18 I just wanted to let you know that I really do think you are amazing. I have an immense amount of love and respect for you. Please be kind to yourself and know that no matter what you wish to talk about or to not talk about, I am here. I hope you enjoy this book. It has played an important role in my life and I hope it touches your heart as it did mine. I don't know many people like you. So giving, so kind and so hilarious. I wish you all the peace and love in the world, you deserve so much.

Ellen xo

21

THE HEALTHY WAY

———

The first girl I kissed worked at the Healthy Way, a smoothie, salad, and sandwich spot in the food court of the Halifax Shopping Centre. I'd returned to Halifax from Toronto to finish high school, taking a beat from acting. Her name was Jessica, and she dressed in all black, her dark, short hair resembling that of Tegan and Sara, a new Canadian band on the scene. Being near her filled me with an anxious excitement. It wasn't so much that I had a crush on her, but that I knew she was queer and I had to be near her because of this. I found myself seeking her out.

I'd ride my bike to the mall solo and order some kind of wrap, watching her hands as she made it. I'd awkwardly say hi, then lose my words, catching a small smile as she grabbed the pickles. I worked to hide mine. Finding an empty table, I'd sit down to eat and then promptly leave without a word, only there to see her and be near her queerness. When I arrived and she wasn't working, there was a mixture of disappointment and relief. Was it a compulsion? I kept going back for those wraps.

Eventually, we hung out one-on-one. I assume Jessica asked me because I was terrified, so nervous I was shaking. The sun had set as we walked down Spring Garden Road toward the harbor, Lord only knows what I was talking about. We stopped just before Barrington Street in front of Saint Mary's Cathedral Basilica, a prodigious stone church that has the tallest granite spire in North America.

She turned around and we stared at each other. We stood close. The Gothic steeple loomed. Silence. She kissed me.

When our lips touched, I short-circuited, the elasticity of my brain not yet able to bend around what was happening. I jerked back, separating my body from hers. My breath became shallow.

"I have to go," I said, "I'm so sorry . . ."

I made a ridiculously obvious excuse.

"Oh, okay," she said. And I promptly fled the scene.

I literally ran away from my first kiss with a girl. Still today I cringe when I think of that moment. I'd been the one going to the food court day after day, watching her carefully place pickles on my sandwich, yet a single kiss made me disintegrate. I left her standing there alone at the foot of the basilica steps. Despite not being religious at all, a small part of me wondered if God had seen. If I had sinned.

Later in the year, after many months of awkward silence and no sandwiches, I went to a party at a classmate's house. Teenagers crowded into the space, drinking and dancing. I saw Jessica. I was buzzed and determined not to be a coward this time. We sat down in the same large chair in the corner of the living room. A big yellow Lab kept coming to say hi. Something was different. I was different. I didn't crumble or shake. And this time when we kissed, it wasn't brief. I did not pull away, but pushed in. My tongue found hers, exploring, moving with the music, dancing in our mouths. I felt her hand reaching for the top button of my jeans.

"Is this okay?"

"Yes," I answered with a nod.

She slid her fingers down my pants and touched me.

"You're so wet," she said.

And I was. Turned on in a way that was new, I felt the sensation I had only managed to reach on my own until this point. My body quivered, I wish we'd been alone, but the presence of others snapped us out of it.

Being in proximity to Jessica changed me. Growing up with hardly any queers around, this person helped me discover myself, someone who had pushed through the fear and the shame to exist proudly. Running into her on the sidewalk, seeing her at a party, eating the wraps she made at the mall, I didn't have a crush, but I yearned to be near what was possible. Her visibility meant the world to me.

I think about this as I walk through the world now.

22

FLATLINERS

———

"You'll be fine," the stunt coordinators said to us.

"It'll be even better if you aren't strapped in," someone said to Kiersey.

We should have removed ourselves, called someone, said something, but we'd been conditioned, filming is extremely costly and you have limited hours, especially during an action-filled night shoot like this one. The sun will come.

It was the summer of 2016, on the precipice of that horrid election. I was filming the remake of the 1980s cult classic *Flatliners,* in which a group of five medical students perform a high-risk experiment. They stop their hearts briefly to induce near-death experiences, "flatlining" until their colleagues resuscitate them. Obviously, things get messy. The original starred Julia Roberts, Kiefer Sutherland, and Kevin Bacon. I was fortunate to work with a fantastic cast for the remake—Diego Luna, Nina Dobrev, James Norton, and Kiersey Clemons.

A brilliant cast, a cult classic, it was set to be great. But it went off the rails, one of those movies that is a true mess from the very beginning.

We were getting ready for a car stunt when Kiersey and I realized that everyone had a built-in thick seat belt, except for us. We looked to the various stunt crew members strapping the others in, perplexed, questioning why we weren't being secured for the scene. "Why does everyone else have a safety belt but not us?" we'd inquired.

Kiersey was laid out in the back over Diego. I was perched on James's lap. No restraints, a basic safety measure of the carefully orchestrated, expensive, and elaborate stunt that hadn't been thought through.

Kiersey and I didn't do anything, except comply and get in the car. We did not say anything further. That worry of appearing "difficult."

The scene began with a panicked escape, hospital security in hot pursuit. Barely making it out, we all barge through a heavy door, appearing in an underground parking garage. We sprint to a red Mini and pack in. Marlo (Nina) hits the gas, Jamie (James) is in the passenger seat, and I am on his lap. Ray (Diego) is in the back with Sophia (Kiersey) sprawled over him.

Our reactions in that scene are genuine. The Mini was being driven by a stunt driver who sat in a go-cart sort of thing on the roof of the car. The vehicle was rigged with cameras to capture all of us. And the director did not want us to see the stunt before we did it.

"I don't want to tell you guys about it, I want it to be a surprise, to get real reactions," he said. We were initially excited. We'd never seen stunt rigging like that, with a person attached to the top of the car. I still don't even know how that works.

I love a thrill. I am a die-hard roller-coaster enthusiast, a *force you to watch POV videos of my fave roller coasters* degree of fanaticism.

I have friends who refer to me as "the mayor of Six Flags Magic Mountain." I would bring people frequently, acting as a guide, the ride order all laid out. You're strapped in at an amusement park, employees walk up and down the rows, checking the various belts and harnesses, pushing and pulling. They yell words indicating all is clear, and off you go. All of those measures making the experience possible, permitting one to surrender. The rise and fall, upside down, backward, the sudden drop, the world whizzes, the body evaporates. It offered respite for almost two minutes, the average length of a roller coaster ride. I could let it all go.

This was different.

At action that car took off at a shocking speed, zooming through the claustrophobic underground garage, barreling toward the gate barrier arm. It did not rise, but smashed against the windshield, the force splintering it. My heart pounded, jaw tight. It jostled the body, shoving it back as the driver barreled up the ramp, taking a hard, sharp turn onto the street right when a car sped past. The Mini swerved, the two left wheels going over the median curb. The vehicle tilted, all of us propelled to the right. I placed my hands firmly on the front dash, attempting to brace myself. Flailing, I had no control, Kiersey and I both. Half the car off the street, we raced by traffic. Our bodies jarred when it pounded back to the cement. The Mini reached the end of the median and pulled a one-eighty. Spinning rapidly, we clasped what we could, inertia taking over.

The director yelled, "Cut!" We sat there in shock. The first take was a whirlwind, a degree of intensity we did not *quite* anticipate. Kiersey and I looked at each other, speechless, staring at our shaking hands. We should have spoken up immediately, but we hadn't. The set pressure, all the moving parts, as if it can never stop.

We got in the car for the second take. James wrapped his arms tighter around my waist. The others had their harnesses double-checked. ACTION. Again, the red Mini hurtled up the ramp, turned right onto the Toronto street, and as the stunt driver went to drive onto the curb, he unexpectedly slammed on the brake, propelling us forward and thrusting us back hard. Someone had driven onto the closed set, a large chunk of a Toronto street that had been blocked off for the nightlong multivehicle car chase. Just a random car in the midst.

Luckily everyone was fine, but I think back to how reckless and dangerous that was. How Kiersey and I were treated with such flippancy and disrespect. Regardless of a stranger's car making it onto the closed set of a car chase, what if something just . . . went wrong?

Kiersey and I have since spoken of this incident many times, turning over why we didn't speak up sooner and more forcefully.

In retrospect, I should have known the shoot was going to be a shitshow. Within our first week, someone approached Kiersey on set, sitting in her chair between takes, *you only have this part because you're Black, you know,* he said to her.

For myself, I knew from the initial wardrobe fitting. Instantly I discerned what they were aiming for. *More like a girl.* Heels and skirts were laid out, which I didn't understand, they were medical students in residency at an intensive care unit. The film takes place over a matter of days, and my character hardly even changes her clothes. I understood the assignment and I was going to comply, but there was categorically no rationale for the character to wear heels or a skirt. I said yes to fancy blouses, tight jeans, and boots with a heel. I figured the issue was settled. We solved the problem, the problem being me.

A day or two later Kiersey, Nina, James, Diego, and myself met for a table read. We gathered in a small, bare conference room in a hotel frequented by members of the film industry because it has corporate suites with small kitchens. We combed through the script, digging into scenes and bonding, the adrenaline at the beginning of a project is always a rush. The sensation of no turning back.

As we were wrapping up, one of the heads of production asked me, "Ellen, can you stay for a bit so we can chat?"

"Sure," I responded, thrown off by his tone, saying goodbye to everyone.

I sat across from him, a desk between us, the sterile room enclosed by unadorned walls.

"You know, Ellen, I grew up in a very progressive area," he began. "It is very open there and I grew up knowing gay people . . ."

Oh no, I thought. *Never a good start.* The words came out as if rehearsed. I imagined him workshopping the moment, blocking it out in his mind, matching the words with the smiles. The cloak of "nice."

"Ellen, are you mad that this character isn't gay?" he asked me.

I stared at him. I paused, less shock, more astonishment. He'd been friendly, grounded, and passionate, someone I was looking forward to working with. His exuberance clear at the table read, I had admired his energy. My astonishment morphed into a quiet boil.

"Are you asking me this because I did not want to wear a skirt?" His face remained the same, an annoying grin with a glinting youthfulness in the eyes, but I pressed on. "Are you really asking me if I am angry about this character not being gay because I am not wearing a fucking skirt?"

He looked on inscrutably, as if being pleasant means you are not queerphobic.

"Your view of women is egregiously narrow," I said to the man, reminding him lesbians wear skirts, too.

He tried to voice a response, fumbling again and again, tripping over his words. He attempted to recover but failed.

I left him in the room and headed back to the studio. When I arrived, I beelined to an executive's office, a man I would later watch give a woman an unwanted massage on set. His subsequent texts to Kiersey asking her to go to dinner glared with gross.

I entered the room with his name on the door and crossed to the chair in front of his desk. I lifted my hands, and curling my fingers I brought them together, creating a nanoscopic tunnel to peer through.

"Your view of women is *this* small." I spied through the hole at him, apoplectic. "It is this fucking small."

He looked back vacuously. I persisted, speaking of the limitations, the misogyny, the queerphobia. All that I had swallowed for years, I hauled out my insides for him to gorge on.

In spite of all that, I continued to prioritize the needs of everyone else over mine. I allowed the erasure, endorsing their disillusionment, trying not to be "difficult" anymore. I knew those in charge were dancing around the subtext. I knew they wanted me to look "less queer." I asked them to leave me to it, again reiterating that if I were to wear the clothes they wished for, I would look ridiculous, incongruous with the script, and that I understood the mission. That I would execute it.

I'm sorry who I am is repulsive.

I'm trying. Can't you see?

I try to rid myself of my "queer walk," the way my
    arms dangle and bend, how my hands move, that
    way I sit, "not ladylike," as my father used to say.
Soften the voice, be quiet.
The screen can't be full of my repugnant features.
    Those "boyish" ones, those "lesbian" ones. I know
    that.
I've known that.

A couple days later, I was at the studio for a screen test, not to be confused with auditions—more like camera tests. You show up to work as if it is a regular day. You head to hair and makeup, discuss looks, what to start with, the character arcs and whatnot. I would sit and face the mirror, eyeliner and mascara being applied, my reflection an enigma. I didn't want to look, because I wasn't there, and the hope that perhaps one day I would be had vanished.

As a child and an adult, I would press my face against my bathroom mirror. The last time I did this was in my trailer while shooting the second season of *The Umbrella Academy*. My eyes opened wide, as close as possible, I would stare, periodically offering butterfly kisses. I could block myself out, I was a person I didn't know, I'd gaze into what felt like the universe, my eye a planet of its own. *I must be somewhere in there,* I'd think.

I changed into my wardrobe, the various outfits we'd finally settled on ready to go. I walked over from base camp to set, meeting many of the crew for the first time. The space already lit. I stood on my mark and spun slowly as instructed. Front. Slow turn. Profile. Slow turn. Back. Slow turn. Other profile. Slow turn. Front. Lens change. A wide to a medium, spin again, a medium to a close-up, spin again.

I stood in front of the camera, waiting as they made minor adjustments, I was enjoying making small talk with the crew members I was meeting for the first time. Of course not loving the clothes, but it was a balancing act I could handle. I was relieved that was settled, that I stood up for myself. That I hadn't just swallowed it.

A producer approached me, all smiles, with his phone out. He lifted it to my face, revealing photos of . . . me. He began to scroll through Google images, slowly moving through, as if I had never seen myself, which I suppose in some ways was true. All the photos had one thing in common: long, wavy hair.

I imagined his fingers typing, "Ellen Page with long hair."

"The studio was thinking hair extensions. They think the long hair just makes you look more . . . soft."

"That sounds like code to me, that really sounds like code to me," I retorted.

My hair was shoulder-length, not even that short. The character was not "soft," nor should she have looked "soft," whatever that even means.

"The studio just thinks . . ." He looked back to the phone. Scrolling down, images of my face, its long hair, makeup, lashes surrounding the eyes, enhancing the emptiness. A slideshow, a mood board for that "soft" and "pretty" look they craved.

"I know what I look like," I said, and I walked off. I'd never walked off before. I wish I had left the project then and there. Instead I called my then agent, who understood and was furious with them. I was grateful for this, to feel seen, not told to shrug it off. It almost never crossed my mind that I could walk away, or that I could call someone, just pick up the phone and say, "This isn't okay." Too many times those who were supposed to protect me did nothing, or if anything, only furthered my silence.

23

U-TURN

——

I'd always been told I was gay, made fun of for being a dyke. I felt more comfortable in environments with queer women, but inherently something in me knew that I was transgender. Something I had always known but didn't have the words for, wouldn't permit myself to embrace.

"I was never a girl, I'll never be a woman. What am I going to do?" I used to say. Have always said.

The first time I acknowledged I was trans, in the properly conscious sense, beyond speculation, was around my thirtieth birthday. Almost four years before I came out as trans publicly.

"Do you think I'm trans?" I'd asked a close friend. They answered hesitantly, knowing no one can come to that conclusion for someone else, but they looked at me with a quiet recognition and said, "I could see that . . ." A sturdiness shining through, a light from under the door.

Then there was the time where I wasn't the one to bring it up. I was having a small party, people jumped in the pool and huddled together on outdoor furniture. My friend Star and I sat off alone, catching up on the patio. I'd met Star while filming the first season of *Gaycation,* our fourth episode being set in the United States.

We interviewed Star in San Francisco at a clinic run by trans women where she worked offering health care and support for those in the LGBTQ+ community who don't have access to such resources. The clinic has since had to move; Twitter bought the block.

Star and I connected, in that way where the future flashes, an auspicious beginning. We stayed in touch, became good friends. Star has experienced far more obstacles and barriers than I have, yet she holds space for me, supports me, sees me. I remember being mesmerized by her voice when I first listened to her eponymous album, *Star*. The lyrics of her song "Heartbreaker" were on repeat in my mind for weeks after:

> I run away from feeling too good
> I'm scared as hell you'd leave me if you knew
> I run away from feeling too good
> I'm scared as hell you'd leave me if you knew

We sat together on an oversize chair, the splashes and music blending together in the background. We spoke about gender, I shared the degree of my discomfort, how even when I was playing a role, I couldn't wear feminine clothes anymore. How I always struggled in the summer when layers were not an option and the presence of my breasts under my T-shirt forced me to incessantly crane my neck, sneaking quick peeks down. I would pull on my shirt, my posture folded. Walking down the sidewalk, I'd glance at a store window to check my profile, my brain consumed. I had to avoid my reflection. I couldn't look at pictures, because I was never there. It was making me sick. I didn't want to be here. I wanted to be lifted out—the gender dysphoria slowly crushing me.

"It's a role, you're an actor. Why are you complaining about such a thing?" people would say.

"I would wear a skirt," a straight, cis man had said to me, playing devil's advocate. I kept trying to explain the difficulty I was having. But he kept spitting out his unwanted opinions while then berating me for getting "too emotional." "Hysterical" I believe was the word he used.

These words triggered a deep shame I'd held since I could remember. I was puzzled, too—invalidating my own experience. How was I in so much pain? Why did even slightly feminine clothing make me want to die? I'm an actor, there shouldn't be a problem. How could I be such an ungrateful prick?

Imagine the most uncomfortable, mortifying thing you could wear. You squirm in your skin. It's tight, you want to peel it from your body, tear it off, but you can't. Day in and day out. And if people are to learn what is underneath, who you are without that pain, the shame would come flooding out, too much to hold. The voice was right, *you deserve the humiliation. You are an abomination. You are too emotional. You're not real.*

"Do you think you're trans?" Star asked me, locking eyes.

"Yes, well, maybe. I think so. Yeah." We exchanged a soft smile.

I was so near. Almost touching it, but I panicked. And it burned away like the joint I was smoking, becoming an old roach left to rot in a forgotten ashtray. It all felt too big—the thought of going through this publicly, in a culture that is so rife with transphobia and people with enormous power and platforms actively attacking the community.

The world tells us that we aren't trans but mentally ill. That I'm too ashamed to be a lesbian, that I mutilated my body, that I will always be a woman, comparing my body to Nazi experiments. It is not trans people who suffer from a sickness, but the society that fosters such hate. As actress and writer Jen Richards once put it:

> It's exceedingly surreal to have transitioned ten years ago, find myself happier & healthier than ever, have better relationships with friends & family, be a better and more engaged citizen, and yes, even more productive . . . and to then see strangers pathologize that choice. My being trans almost never comes up. It's a fact about my past that has relatively little bearing on my present, except that it made me more empathetic, more engaged in social justice. How does it hurt anyone else? What about my peace demands vitriol, violence, protections?

Sitting with Star by the pool, I couldn't quite touch the truth, but I could talk about my gender without bawling. That was a step. It had taken a long time to allow any words to come out. When the subject came up in therapy, my reaction felt inordinate, lost in sobs.

"Why do I feel this way?" I'd plead. "What is this feeling that never goes away? How can I be desperately uncomfortable all the time? How can I have this life and be in such pain?"

Not long after my thirtieth birthday, I did a U-turn, I bailed, I stopped talking about it. I closed my eyes and hid it away. Somewhere I'd never find it. It would be four more years until I disclosed who I was.

I met my ex-spouse, Emma, around the same time. Meeting Emma let me leave it behind, a foggy memory. Falling madly in love, the energy was indisputable, just a hug would make my body shake. I threw myself in, and we got married quickly.

If a part of you is always separate, if existing in your body feels unbearable—love is an irresistible escape. You transcend, a sensation so indescribable that philosophers, scientists, and writers can't seem to agree on what the fuck it even is—if it even is. I often wonder if I have actually experienced deep love. I feel as though I have, but is it real if you were never there? When you have numbed yourself to the truth?

Love was unwittingly an emotional disguise, and my relationship to it is another muscle to be transformed. I don't want to disappear. I want to exist in my body, with these new possibilities. Possibilities. Perhaps that is one of the main components of life lost to lack of representation. Options erased from the imagination. Narratives indoctrinated that we spend an eternity attempting to break. The unraveling is painful, but it leads you to you.

During my marriage I ignored therapy, and when we moved to New York City from Los Angeles at the end of 2018, I virtually stopped going to therapy altogether. It wasn't until our relationship was falling apart two years later and my gender dysphoria so extreme that I sought out someone in the city. I was ready to talk.

I could barely find the words, but I did. As if they moved on their own, wriggling through and up my body, pouring out. My body knew, deep down I knew, and something had shifted. It was now or never. It was alive or not.

24

YOUR HEAVENLY DADDY

———

In the aftermath of coming out as gay in 2014, I wrote a list in my head of experiences I was unable to have before, certain activities that, regardless of desire, felt important to embrace. I had a burgeoning sense of ease in the world, a confidence. It was not ultimately where I needed to be, but I felt brave, properly so, for the first time in a long time. At that point in my life, it didn't really feel like a choice, there was no other option. I had to choose to engage as my authentic self, or die not trying. There was a swell from somewhere else, inside, but beneath it all—a voice. One that would whisper again close to seven years later.

This is your life. You don't need to believe their stories. Those are their narratives. This is your career. Why are you agreeing with them? Trusting them? They aren't the right ones. They, in fact, are wrong. You don't believe them. This isn't a dress rehearsal. This is your life.

Not long before my heart was shredded by "Ryan," I saw the superb, painful, and infuriating documentary *God Loves Uganda,* a film by the astounding Roger Ross Williams. The doc examined the role of American evangelicalism in Uganda, its ties to a recently introduced bill, the Uganda Anti-Homosexuality Act—which then suggested the death penalty for LGBTQ+ people—as it gained serious momentum. It follows missionaries, evangelical leaders, and the LGBTQ+ people of Uganda who fight for their right to exist.

These activists were standing up against vicious oppression, rhetoric, and ideas originally introduced and continuously perpetuated by the West. Concealed in "good deeds," American missionaries created infrastructure for access to indoctrinate the populace, which fueled anti-LGBTQ+ violence and hate. These activists should not have to be doing this work, but the reality is that they have no other option, they can't rest. They face extreme and brutal consequences, in large part because of the exportation of American evangelical anti-LGBTQ+ religious and social doctrine. It is true for those who are the most vulnerable in the States as well, it is simply disguised better. To some, people like me being on the cover of major magazines must mean things are all good. *What could they possibly be complaining about?* Pink washing works.

Ellen, look how much these people risk, how much they face. You're a coward, I scolded myself. I felt I needed to call myself out for the selfish little shit I could be, especially when it is to maintain comfort and privilege. Perhaps I am being harsh on myself, because the road was extremely challenging, it did almost run me out, I was terrified and bloated with self-disgust. I can hold that *and* also understand just how good I have it, and knowing just how good should only enlighten the need for action, for care, to make the right choices, the uncomfortable choices. Stepping up is not just for the individual, and I am able to be out because of countless other people, ones who did not have access to what I have, who won't end up on magazine covers.

You can handle simply telling people you are gay, I told myself.

Coming out was not easy, which is shocking to think now, but I suppose we (or I) forget the degree of change (and lack thereof) that has happened over the past decade. Going from a therapist's office where I believed it impossible to be out as queer to feeling perplexed and furious that I had to deal with the bullshit for so long, that camouflaging my queerness was treated as the norm, my pain as a natural consequence. Pain that did not just live in my mind, but also loitered throughout my entire body, eating it out from the inside, forcing me to the ground.

I've made a habit of requiring a hefty push to the edge, *almost* over, in order to finally address "feelings," and not just that, but also to simply acknowledge there are any. But even in my lowest moments, a piece of me, ever so small, becomes clearer and clearer. An opening, fragile and elusive. Instantly, it comes flooding in. It's fleeting. Seize it. A whisper that sits waiting.

Close your eyes and step through.

After I came out, shockingly enough, the world did not end and my life improved, and now I had that as a reference in my chest pocket. *If you can do that, you have nothing to be afraid of,* I'd mutter to myself.

Once while driving north on the 101 to break up with someone, I listened to my coming-out speech, trying to not shit blood, a reminder—*if you can do that, you have nothing to be afraid of.* Embarrassing, but effective.

This time of firsts and newfound boldness was also, unsurprisingly perhaps, the most promiscuous period of my life.

I had never had a one-night stand. I had barely even slept with people casually. I had never had a blind date, or an out date. I wanted those things, those adventures, even if they were awkward and messy or ill-advised or out of my league. All of a sudden I could magically talk to women, I could flirt, a new self-assurance that I'd been aiming toward, hoping for. I was direct, not concerned with the potential rejection. If I felt timid or hesitant, I simply pushed myself to continue. *Just keep talking. Half smile. A cute silence.*

My first one-night stand has, to this day, been my only one-night stand. She was the first person I slept with after my relationship with Ryan ended. Heartbroken, but numb at this point, I had met up with my friend Shannon at a bar on Sunset Boulevard in Silver Lake, where we typically converged in the compact outdoor area. Vines curled over the top of the tall walls, as did the rising fog from cigarettes. We sipped tequila with a touch of soda and lime. I hoped a tequila or two would enhance my numbness. My friend did not know how badly my heart was broken, I could not tell her. She did not know I had been in a relationship for close to two years.

I slid over to make space for a woman to sit. She had long brown hair and curious, playful eyes that were paired with a mischievous grin.

"Hi," she said as she sat close.

She already seemed a touch tipsy, *leaning in on purpose or not?*

"Hi," I replied, with the tiniest of side smiles.

We began chatting, in that uncontrolled, organic way, where halfway through you catch yourself, puzzled at such ease with a stranger. She was hot, she was flirting, and I was flirting back. Another friend arrived, and soon after, Shannon and she split off, allowing me to turn my full focus to the conversation with my new pal.

We didn't have much in common, but that wasn't really the point and I think we both knew it. We sat progressively closer. Time passed. It was not until I got up to go to the bathroom and to get us another drink when I finally asked her name and shared mine.

"Ryan," she said.

"What?"

"Ryan," she said again.

I thought I misheard, like a quick cutaway in a film—the character imagining. Nope. She had the same exact name. The exact fucking name.

I squeezed between the crowd of hipsters, making my way to the restroom. I stood in line, waiting behind a woman in a cowboy hat who stared down at her phone.

Should I call it? I wasn't sure. We had been talking for a while. She was attractive. I wanted to follow through. I wanted to be spontaneous, I wanted to have what I could not have before . . . but the same name?!

"Of course," I said to no one as I locked the bathroom door, "of course her name is Ryan."

I pulled down my pants and sat. Ruminating as I urinated. *Fuck it,* I decided to shrug it off, roll with it, poetry in action! I flushed the toilet with intent. This was *my* night.

I returned with drinks, but we left before finishing them. Her place was not far west, a two-story condo in an old low building. Built presumably in the 1930s or 1940s, its architecture was distinct, not art deco, not quite Craftsman, definitely quaint. We sat in the living room briefly, she drank straight from a bottle of champagne. No longer amid the cozy buzz of the bar, her energy shifted, she was frenetic, zooming from one topic to the next, pacing about. Only later was I like . . . *oooh cocaine!* I always forget about cocaine.

We went upstairs so she could "show me her room," and the moment we walked through the door, we fell into bed together. Her kissing was fierce, no warm-up, clanging teeth. Clothes started coming off. She was dominant. Her tits were almost immediately in my mouth. I grabbed them, they were perfectly round and soft. I sucked and swallowed and teased her nipples with my tongue. I felt them get hard in my mouth, she started to moan.

Pushing me back on the bed, she lifted the short skirt she had been wearing and climbed on top of me. Riding and grinding, her head was back, arms straight, propping herself up with her hands on my shins. She rose and caught my eyes. She stared down at me with that vacant glare, pupils dilated, looking right through me. Placing her hand on my throat, she squeezed and squeezed as she continued to rub and pound, her coked-up eyes squinted callously.

Now, I don't mind a hand on the throat, some pressure, a squeeze, that's fun. But full-throttle choke? First time? . . . Nah. I didn't say no. I've almost never said no, and times when I have, it didn't do a whole lot, or made things worse. I wanted to stop it but couldn't make a sound—not just because of her hand. It was like a dream where you need to yell but your mouth produces silence, like a dream where you go to run, but your legs remain still, feet locked to the ground. Her hand tightened harder and harder, preventing my breath from flowing until she came on top of me. Loud and distant. Her body folded forward, her head landing on the pillow next to me as she rolled off.

I lay in her bed as she slept until light glowed around the perimeter of the curtains and the new sun guided my way out.

My first properly out date was more successful. We were set up by mutual friends and met at a bar in the Bowery. She looked like Jean Seberg. Her short, crisp blond hair and natural sense of style exuded an ease and elegance, it all felt like an afterthought. We sat inside, engaged in conversation. Life, art, books. As time passed, we crept closer. Such a simple action, a casual chat in a bar, just simply a date. But it was monumental for me—the anxiety, the over the shoulder, the *can they tell?* . . . evaporated.

We stayed until the bar closed. I suggested we get a room at a hotel because I was crashing with a friend. I *know,* a ridiculous splurge for one evening, but this was my first out date! As we walked north up Bowery, we put our arms around each other. Coming at us down the sidewalk, I heard the characteristic calls of some drunk bros calling out to us, to which I responded with a new defiance, "Fuck you!"

Turns out my date was a black belt, and what I should have done was not engage and move on. Like a duck, let it roll off my back. Peacefully extracting oneself from the drama and toxicity instead of throwing kindling on the fire. After we walked away, she showed me self-defense moves on the sidewalk. Demonstrating how, even though small, I could fuck someone up. She flipped me over her back (gently), twisted my arm, made me submit. It was comforting knowing skills were available to me that, despite my size, could render an attacker useless. Educational foreplay! Lifesaving foreplay!

We checked into the Bowery Hotel. It was all so different from being with Ryan. It was thrilling, in fact, a scene in a movie I never thought could play out in real life. With Ryan, we once asked for a cot at the front desk of a hotel when only a room with a single bed was available. With Paula, we would have separate hotel rooms because she was my assistant. *What odd things to do, when this way was a possibility,* I thought.

We sat in the room at a tiny table and talked more. Thick velvet drapes were pushed aside, leaving the old, large windows visible. The city lights filtered in.

"I like your cadence," she said.

Time paused. I swallowed her words, feeling them at the base of my throat, the vibration traveled down. Her voice, smooth and clear with bedroom eyes that I wanted in.

She leaned forward in her chair. Placing her hand on my leg, she kissed me and I kissed her back. We were soon in the bed and stayed there until the morning light greeted us. Awkward at first, as it always is, struggling with buttons, subtle tumbles while removing tight jeans, bodies reading each other, working to connect, to sync, to find that flow. It felt spontaneous and safe and, most important, open. A new world.

We fell asleep, but not for very long. Shockingly, we awakened hungover and hungry. Checking out, I dropped off the golden key with its red tassel at the front desk and said goodbye, and we left in search of food. We found a place around the corner from the hotel for breakfast, a hip, rustic restaurant in a basement on Bond Street.

My first out breakfast with a girl.

Rad.

This used to feel impossible.

Blood sugar up, caffeine in the veins, our new destination was McNally Jackson Books, an independent bookstore on Prince Street in SoHo, only a five-minute walk away. She wanted to get me a book, Maggie Nelson's *Bluets.* This would be the first time I read Maggie Nelson. *Bluets,* a contemplation of Nelson's love of the color blue, feels impossible to categorize—nonfiction, a mixture of memoir, heartbreak, history, philosophy, theory—all of it seamlessly strung together through poetry and prose. It's staggering, heart opening. It was the perfect book to receive then and there.

It started to rain, but that did not stop us. We continued walking and talking until we found ourselves on the other side of Manhattan in the West Village. She suggested a coffee at the now closed Cafe Gitane in the Jane Hotel, a historic hotel on the corner of Jane and West. The café was charming and chill, with a black-and-white checkered floor underfoot. It had a Parisian vibe, intermixed with unique decor choices, such as an alligator on the wall. I sipped an

Americano, my stomach could only handle half. This was the moment we both started to fade, fatigue catching up, we finally brought the date to a close. We stood, said goodbye. And she kissed me. Right there in the café. A first.

These moments were beautiful, however complicated, for their significance in my life.

But the first person I really fell for after having my heart broken was Kate Mara. She had a boyfriend at the time, the lovely and talented Max Minghella. I met them both at a small dinner. That first night, I didn't think much of it. Kate was charming and gorgeous, of course, but she was sitting next to her boyfriend. Mostly, I was eager to follow up with Max, hoping he'd accept a role in a film I was producing and acting in. But then I met Kate a second time.

It was awards season, and a friend, Kiwi Smith, was throwing a party at her house in Los Feliz for Adèle Exarchopoulos, the star of *Blue Is the Warmest Colour*. This is something people do during awards season, they have parties for people and films, inviting members of the Academy, hoping the support will lead to votes. These were the kinds of things I went to every night in dresses and heels and makeup, where older men sat too close and were too drunk and said through beading sweat, "Your dreams are coming true."

This party for Adèle Exarchopoulos wasn't like that though, it was genuine and sincere, like Kiwi. It was to celebrate an actor, an unforgettable performance, to welcome her in a time that must have been overwhelming. In a city that will suck you dry, it was an alcove, not a trap.

I'd been broken up with Ryan for only a few months maybe. We slept together occasionally after breaking up. Of course, it was too complicated and painful, but I kept convincing myself and her that it was totally chill. *It's okay, we can just be present with each other, I'm fine, I want what is best for you and me* . . . a bunch of bullshit. I was a complete mess until it stopped. We hadn't talked in a while.

I missed her something awful. Her smell, that mix of sweat and sunscreen, her smile, the way she moved her hands, how they danced with her thoughts, her brain, her laugh, her elusiveness, her eyebrows, her work ethic, her curiosities, her lips, her sounds, her art, her neck—how it stretched, her nerdiness, her wonder. Her eyes, the way she looked at me. I missed every single damn thing, and I couldn't stop, it wouldn't stop. I was desperate to forget.

"Above all, I want to stop missing you," writes Maggie Nelson in *Bluets*.

I, too, wanted to *Eternal Sunshine of the Spotless Mind* that shit right out of me.

I arrived at Kiwi's, walked through her entryway with its high ceilings and impressive staircase, her smaller, Gothic-esque dining room and her narrow, bright, and beautifully designed kitchen into the backyard. It was bustling with partygoers, with catering and professional bartenders. I scanned the space. Confirmed. I'd be flying solo with my heartbreak, none of my friends at the party knew I had been with Ryan, including Kiwi. I prayed Ryan would not show, despite being the only person I wanted to see. *Not sure I can fake it tonight.*

Kate was standing in a circle of partygoers, chatting, organic. She held a glass of red wine in her right hand. Her profile got me, that jaw. Welcoming me warmly, with a look in her eye I didn't remember from the dinner before, she invited me in. She seemed looser, but not because of the alcohol. Her wine moved about her glass as she spoke, and I wondered if you could consider the liquid's movement inertia. I reminded myself that she had a boyfriend. When she started flirting with me, I thought it was a joke. Regardless of the boyfriend, I could never imagine Kate Mara would want me.

We bantered back and forth, overtly flirtatious. I kept looking over my shoulder at Max, who was close by.

"Oh, he doesn't care," Kate said, noticing.

"Well, come over then, and I'll make you a tofu scramble in the morning." Now only half joking.

She laughed, I could make her laugh. We stood near, shoulders brushing.

Gulp. I looked to Max again.

Our conversation naturally came to a close, the flow and movement of the guests created a shift in migratory patterns. I found myself on the other end of the yard, having a cigarette on a long wooden bench, making basic chitchat with people I had never met. High from the flirtation, but assuming it was nothing, back to boring small talk.

During a moment of pause, completing the last couple puffs, the cigarette having burned to its logo, a man approached. He looked familiar.

"Hi!" the man said enthusiastically while he sat down next to me without asking. "You're one of Ryan's best friends, right?! I'm Matt!"

I looked at him, puzzled. He looked back with a big, annoying, goofy smile. And then it clicked. Something in me sunk, I just knew.

"Oh, are you two . . . ?" I said, gesturing with my hand, implying *together*.

"Yeah! Oh, she didn't mention?"

Fist. To. The. Gut. Ears. Ring. Heart. Stop. Now.

Breath.

"Oh, I didn't um . . . how long have you . . . ?" (same hand gesture).

"One month! I'm in love with her, she's in love with me." His body bounced on the bench. "Have you ever been in love?"

I looked to the ground, the world moved away like a k-hole. *Who the fuck asks that?*

He kept speaking. He sounded like the adults in *Peanuts*.

I tried to not cry, to offer a smile, not *too* much though, and periodically, I gave a tiny nod.

"Where is she? She coming tonight?" I asked without looking.

"Nah, she was exhausted from meetings all day, she's on her way to my place now."

Fist. To. The. Gut. Ears. Ring. Heart. Stop. Now.

Breath.

"Sorry, I have to go to the bathroom. Nice to meet you, I'm sure I'll see you around." I left him there, basking in his euphoria—as vivid and vibrant as his tie-dye hoodie.

Panic swelling, vision blurred, no one at the party to turn to, I ran into the small half bath on the main floor. I sat on the toilet and immediately started shitting. I felt it in every part of my body. The grief, the shame. Dirt swept under the rug, left behind, but not fully disposed of.

I stared at myself in the mirror (never helpful). And then I left the party. I was sober, I had driven, my hands floated, separate from the rest, odd little aliens on the wheel. I shat it out, now I'd leave, just float above.

When home, I put on a Leonard Cohen record (not helpful) and smoked up the chimney (properly harmful). Why when hurting do we want to perpetuate the pain? Self-punishment?

Managing to hydrate at least, I went to the kitchen for water. My phone dinged—an email from Kate.

Wow, thank you for such a romantic goodbye.

I chuckled. A smile stayed on my face longer than was appropriate. I clicked Reply.

It was too painful to say goodbye.

Head on the pillow, I thought of him going home to her. I thought of her waiting for him.

Above all, I want to stop missing you.

I eventually fell asleep.

Kate and I kept talking. I was starting to sense our flirtation was not just a half-truth, for both of us. We spoke of getting together for a walk or maybe a dinner around our birthdays? We were Pisces buds.

It was a couple weeks later, on Valentine's Day, that I came out as gay. I barely told anyone I was about to make that speech. I just wanted it to be mine, for myself, tired of gossip and speculation. The response was significant, it went "viral," as the kids say.

Kate emailed.

Wait. You're gay?!

Me.

Yeah, so make your move.

The day after I came out as gay, I flew to Montreal for brief reshoots on *X-Men: Days of Future Past.*

"You seem so different," a producer remarked.

It was true, I had left a bag of bricks behind. More in my body, head high. Affable, less troubled, a break from the furrowed brow. I was on my way.

On my flight back to Los Angeles a few days later, I settled into my seat as a priest and his curate walked past, their seats were behind me. The curate recognized me, he was very kind and complimentary. I wasn't expecting that.

I fell asleep on and off, read a script. A couple hours into the flight I felt a tap on my left shoulder. It was the priest and the curate, they passed me a piece of folded loose-leaf paper. A note. I smiled pleasantly and turned around to read it.

I unfolded it, expecting a kind message from an LGBTQ+ supporting, progressive religious leader.

No dice.

It began with him acknowledging that his companion knew who I was, but he did not.

> *I took the liberty of googling you.* (Uh-oh)

He went on to say that what I am wasn't real. A belief and just that.

> *Your soul is struggling. You need the arms of the Heavenly Father around you.* (Ew)

And I kid you not.

> *Signed,*
> *Your Heavenly Daddy.*

There were a couple hours left on the flight. I was not sure what to do. *Do I say something? Do I write a note back?* I figured, what was the point? Truly. A quick convo is not going to change that priest's mind, and giving any of it the time of day would let the toxins sink in. So, I refolded the note, stuck it in my pocket, and went back to my business. The plane landed. Welcome home.

A month or so later, Kate invited me to a BBQ at her and Max's house at the top of a Silver Lake peak. Max had said yes to being in *Into the Forest,* I was excited to see him and celebrate, he'd be playing my love interest. Their place felt like a home. Cozy, nicely designed, personal. The living room had the kind of couch you want to disappear into. It was white, and I had no idea how they managed to keep it pristine. I get stains over everything. The kitchen was small, seemingly unchanged since the house was built in the 1930s. The sink, the backsplash, all perfect. Out a door from the kitchen was a sprawling, steep backyard. A deck off the living room, a firepit down below, and an area for her two Boston terriers.

We hugged, a long one. Introductions took place, I knew almost no one at the party. Kate and Max barbecued veggie burgers and regular burgers. Kate and I sat next to each other on the steps that connected the house to the firepit.

We sat close, flirting. Max stood nearby, not giving it a second look. Magnetic and immediate, a feeling better left without words.

A couple days later we finally hung out one-on-one. I drove to her house to go for a walk. We climbed in her SUV with her dogs in the back and headed down to the Silver Lake Reservoir. It was the same. Smiles you try to hide. Avoiding the eyes.

We pulled into her garage, and she turned off the car. Sitting in silence for a few beats, a telepathic touch.

"We should get dinner soon," Kate said.

I paused.

"I don't think we should go to dinner," I replied. Which was my way of saying *I think we should go to dinner*.

Another pause. Car airtight.

"I can ask Max, talk to him about it, I really don't think he would have a problem."

My chin moved to my chest as I attempted to hide a smile. I was not expecting to hear this, but it was all I wanted to hear. An unmistakable feeling, electric and warm. I yearned to be near her.

"Well, if Max is fine with it, then fuck yeah," I said.

He was. Totally fine with it, supportive of Kate exploring her connection with me.

So, we planned a date for the following week, a dinner in West Hollywood.

Kate came to my house first. When I opened the door, she had that look, that smile, a glare that is simultaneously sweet and assertive. Our lips met for the first time, a shiver, my knees were ready to snap, our tongues spiraled as we swayed toward the couch.

Kate pulled away.

"Not yet, let's go have dinner first," she said.

We headed up Laurel, over Mulholland, down toward West Hollywood. The Uber took a right at the corner where Ryan's poster had stared at me for the first time. Having been distracted during Kate's initial arrival, I could fully see her now, streetlights shining in. The yellows and reds, a glow around her, incandescent. Her dirty-blond hair sparkled subtly in the passing beams. Her tight black pants squeezed her thighs, I avoided looking down. She wore a gray T with a button-down open under a black jacket.

If you had seen us, you would have thought it just a regular date.

How we touched, how we stared, how we laughed too much. Salads and french fries and tequila and wine. She had such presence, assertive posture, just a wink made the room disappear.

That night the paparazzi took photos of us while we were getting in an Uber to return to my place. It was as if I were in another dimension, all the anxiety of being "caught" was no longer. When we got back, we immediately went to my bedroom. Kate lay on her back, removing her clothes, while I stood at the base of the bed removing mine. I moved to crawl on top of her. Our mouths fused, our bodies meeting for the first time. Kissing her neck, I placed my hand on her inner thigh, slowly moving my fingers up.

It was a successful first date. So they continued.

We'd hang with mutual friends or go to a party, and people assumed we were together. There was no shame or hiding, just unabashed attraction. I knew quickly it wasn't *just* lust, chemicals bouncing around, there was deep care. Still is. We love each other.

After our first couple of dates, I knew I was falling. I could not stop thinking about her. The flash of a memory that catches, making you laugh out of nowhere in your car on the way to a meeting. Starting and stopping texts. Preoccupied by a word choice for seventy-two hours. That person who comes to mind.

An earthquake skyrocketed me out of bed one morning, not long after our first date. My heart leaped from my body. My brain told me to go stand in a doorframe, so I did, which it turns out you are not supposed to do. Nonetheless, I waited for the shaking to subside and breathed a sigh of relief. Now I know what to do, here is what the CDC says, so we are all on the same page:

If you are able, seek shelter under a sturdy table or desk. Stay away from outer walls, windows, fireplaces, and hanging objects. If you are unable to move from a bed or chair, protect yourself from falling objects by covering up with blankets and pillows.

When everything calmed, pulse returning to a steady beat, I picked up my phone. My first instinct was to text Kate, to see if she was okay, which caught me off guard. It felt a little much, this was all brand-new, and I reminded myself of the boyfriend and my responsibility to not be an asshole. Ready to put some coffee on, I set down my cell and walked to the kitchen. PING! I turned back to look, it was Kate, she was making sure I was okay. I stared at the text, out came my unprompted, soft chuckle again. *Fuck*.

There is a moment I will never forget, where it sunk in, when it went somewhere else. Spike Jonze invited us to a double birthday party. Held in an old school, it was Spike's friend's fiftieth and his pal's daughter's sixteenth. The main level had an auditorium, which was for the adults. A live band played, people danced and drank. Those brown-and-beige school colors gave the night a timeless sheen.

Arm in arm we went up to the roof, which was the sixteenth-birthday zone. A tall chain-link fence enclosed the rooftop basketball court, and teenagers stood about. A DJ was set up playing sick tunes, but none of the kids were dancing, not one. I imagined they were discussing how to get alcohol, or whatever it is teenagers do in Los Angeles.

The DJ was more our vibe than the downstairs band. Beyoncé, Missy Elliott . . . we dove in without speaking. Lost in movement, Kate, the only thing in focus. Nothing but us. We stared directly, unshakable, bodies feeding off each other, saying what words could not. The dancing, more intimate than touch, was shameless and unreserved. I'd never seen Kate that unconstrained. I felt the universe split open. And myself with it. I was a goner.

A week later, we sat on the lawn on the northeast side of the Silver Lake Reservoir, immersed in our bubble, jotting down notes in a small Moleskine. We thought it was a fantastic idea to make a film together, specifically a love story. Kate and I emailed our agents about finding something for us to do together.

The wheels were set in motion. Quickly we were sent a script by Joe Barton. It was short, only eighty-something pages, it needed work and expanding, but the skeleton of a painful but beautiful film was there. Joe Skyped with us, a lovely Brit who wrote queer female characters with such nuance I was shocked. We discussed story, the characters, and what we felt needed elaboration.

"I wrote that script so long ago. Give me a month and I will come back with a new draft," Joe said.

And he did, taking the script to a whole new level, and the project started to develop.

Time away from Kate started to hurt. Electric and elated, flying high in the moment, but always an end. The places we couldn't go. The places I should not have been wishing for. Friends would encourage me to step back, rightfully so, *again* someone is unavailable. Even now that I was out, I found something to get in the way.

"You remind me of my friends who only date married men," a friend said to me. Chasing the high, coming down, searching for it again.

Later, the same friend saw us as a duo in the flesh, and got it, which was validating and annoying. The love was tangible, we glowed together.

But Max. Max! Max. A truly delightful human, he has been nothing but wonderful to me. Kate loved him, how could she not? But whatever was happening between us was finding new language, it seeped through the cracks. Well, I was letting it. I shouldn't have. I was the one entering a situation involving a serious relationship.

The first time I was struck with a pain too sharp was when Kate and I were supposed to have time in New York City together, but schedules were altered and Max came with her. I'd been anticipating a delightful romantic couple of days in NYC. It hurt. It really hurt. But again, I took it as being on me, the side piece.

I was there doing press for *X-Men: Days of Future Past,* a film where I spent almost all of it sitting behind Hugh Jackman, an unconscious Wolverine, with my hands held on either side of his head, hovering by his temples. A lovely place to be every day, Hugh Jackman is so fucking nice it is annoying, one of the kindest people I've ever worked with, literally never have I seen him in a bad mood.

But after this news from Kate, I was in a pretty bad mood. When I saw paparazzi photos of them walking around the city, I was in a worse mood. And when I thought of them fucking, well. I was doing an interview with Josh Horowitz when a fan question from someone named Kate asked what I thought about bananas. It referenced an inside joke we had together. Kate was friends with Josh and thought this would be funny. It took a second, then I got it. It wasn't comical to me. I was in pain, missing her.

I was angry. Pissed. It felt manipulative. This was a pattern I was familiar with, that I perpetuated and shamed myself for. I found myself blaming her: *if she couldn't be with me, she'd manage to find another way to enter my field, my mind.* I'd always get sucked back in, convincing myself it was healthy, convincing myself that my yearning wasn't slowly chipping away at my integrity. I did not feel I was being treated thoughtfully, my feelings weren't being considered. I unfairly assumed she could read my mind. I was saying, "all good, of course," but I was asking her to interpret it as the opposite.

I probably should have bounced at this point, for many reasons. Mostly to be a good person and respect their relationship, but I was not feeling like a very good person, more like a selfish person who wanted someone. But a genuine connection, like the one we had, is rare and difficult to walk away from. I sat in my hotel room at the Bowery, smoking a cigarette on the balcony, Kate and I had been in this room before. I couldn't help the flashes of her lifting me naked onto the desk, fucking me while she watched my ass in the mirror.

Everything with Kate was becoming more complicated, more loaded. I was feeling let down. Perhaps the excitement no longer outweighed the challenges. It was my choice to enter the situation, my decision to not take care of my heart, but to remain, ignoring the fissure as it grew. I was chasing something that could not be, letting lust overwhelm me.

This dynamic was familiar. Alone you thrive, secret and safe, but separate you feel invisible. It's there and then it is gone, not even a second thought, but an afterthought. I was projecting this onto her, a pattern and a narrative that would take me time to shake—*please love me*.

Kate sensed my pain, the heartache, the last thing she wanted to do was hurt me. Kate was away working but made time to talk. I told her about the agony I had felt in New York.

"I was missing you so much, beyond excited to see you and then I couldn't. I didn't get to see you and I barely heard from you and then you do *that,*" I said, in reference to the interview. "It made me feel like shit."

"I get it, I'm so sorry, I just thought it would be funny." She paused. A moment of still on the screen. "I miss you, too. It hurt not to see you, too."

And at that, the floodgates opened. I started to cry and then she joined in and we spoke of everything. Our love for each other, how organic and meaningful it felt, the depth of care.

"But I love Max, too, and we have a life together," she said. "I didn't believe someone could love two people at the same time before. I do now."

We shared a sadness, the grief in letting go, but first and foremost we cared about having a future, however that looked, forming a new kind of relationship. We decided to take space, no correspondence for at least a month.

I always need to remind myself just how beneficial space can be. It can be agonizing, even if you are the one who initiates it. It is so easy to trick ourselves. I'd convince myself communication was fine, healthy, mature. Yet no matter how much my brain understood, those feelings would lurk and disguise, whisper and poke, my heart jonesing for more.

"You remind me of my friends who only date married men." I understand this more now.

It is true, desperate for the serotonin bump and then wallowing in the pain of rejection. Ultimately abandoning myself in the process, evanesce, which perhaps is what we are looking for, safer to have love unfulfilled, to yearn for those unavailable.

Max and Kate ended their relationship not long afterward and shortly before I would be filming with Max. The breakup wasn't about Kate wanting to be with me, but a mutual understanding that it was time to move on. Kate and I kept the space going. Max was nothing but wonderful to me, superb in the film, a generous and present actor to work with. We had a sex scene, one of the more intimate ones I have done, both of us practically naked, my chest on display. It felt safe and easy, not strange, despite it being, frankly, strange.

I still had feelings for Kate, desired her, wanted to be with her. The distance helped. I felt like I had just about let it go, but we found ourselves both back in LA, and the same city stirred the heart once again. I was confused, dejected, resentful even. *She could be with me now. But she doesn't want to be with me now.*

"Love doesn't constitute a relationship," as my therapist would say.

Once again, I was in pain. Anger was squirreling its way out.

Minutes crawled and healed. It helped not talking or texting. I slowly started to unhook, to reflect, to be accountable. My fixation removed, I was able to date properly, to meet women who were available and out. Friends set up Samantha and me, we were together for about two years. She visited me in Ohio on the outskirts of Cincinnati when I was making *My Days of Mercy* with Kate, the film we produced and starred in together. Sam was supportive, not jealous, the three of us went to an Amy Schumer show in Kentucky just across the border. Kate was dating Jamie, now her husband.

Considering the situation, the shoot went well.

It has been nearly nine years since Kate and I met. Certain chemistry never faded, but room for realizations left us laughing at how little we had in common. In retrospect, we'd mostly been fucking. But what has never changed, what will never change, is the love between us. Loyal, generous, emotionally present—Kate is not just a wonderful friend, she is an honest friend.

My tendency was to fantasize, not look or respond to what was actually happening. I did not *listen*. And, to put it bluntly, I was codependent. Only now am I finally moving away from that. Better boundaries, less fearful, more openhearted. Stronger, with a bur-geoning confidence I did not possess before. Reminders and lessons emerge from our most painful moments, ones I'm sure I will forget and have to remember again. But I would rather remember, I'd rather the hurt than not—at least I got to love you, at least I felt your love for me. Maggie Nelson:

> That this blue exists makes my life a remarkable one,
> just to have seen it. To have seen such beautiful things.
> To find oneself placed in their midst. Choiceless.

25

CHOOSING FAMILY

———

"I just want to live with you," I said to my mother at thirteen, "I don't want to go back and forth anymore."

No longer did I want to count the days down to the sixteenth, I wanted to live with my mom full-time.

Her eyes lit up, her posture straightened, I could see the excitement. She worked to conceal her joy, presumably to not influence my decision. I could tell she was happy, which made me happy. Her face went from a big grin to more focused, she wondered why I wanted to make the change?

Nervous, I stumbled on my words. Looking down, I scrounged for a reason, wishing I didn't need one as guilt clawed at me.

"I just want to be in one place. I am tired of going back and forth. I'm always forgetting stuff."

Telling her the whole truth about how I felt in that house seemed impossible. An inexplicable fear pulsated within me, holding me back. I was too afraid to cause an upheaval that would never be restored.

The bitterness had reached a peak, a thick fog in the house when

I got home from school and found myself alone with Linda. I'd even ask a pal who came over, Did they sense it, too?

"Her vibe is weird, right?" I said. Her energy. That tone. Those looks. "I don't think she likes me." They agreed.

I didn't have friends over much. I wondered what my soccer teammates thought on the rare occasions they came over. As my dad used to "jokingly" catcall them from the car while they walked home from junior high school.

"Heeeey there, looking good, ladies!" he'd yell.

"Ewww, Dennis!" they'd respond. Not quite laughing. I'd hide and cringe in the passenger seat.

My father changed, depending on who was around. With Linda he would shut down with me, but alone with me, he shared deep love, blurring emotional boundaries. Perhaps this was the only way he knew how to remain close, scavenging for connection when he could and protecting it, ours alone.

In any event, I didn't have the words for it at the time and I still struggle with them. I was running on ice, just hoping for the dirt's friction.

I asked my mother to not tell my dad yet, my stomach clamped tight at the thought of it. How upset he would be, how hurt. The guilt continued to roam through me.

"Your father will understand," my mom said in a comforting tone. It is not that she believed he would be devoid of hurt, of course it would sting, but that ultimately he would support my decision despite it.

I knew this was not true. I knew that he would not understand. I knew he'd be furious. Face turned sharp. But I did not know how to express this to my mother.

That evening I had a soccer match. Passing the ball back and forth, Tina and I warmed up on the Dalhousie University turf, a home game for us. A midfielder, right wing, I wanted to focus on the corner kick coming, timing and bending the run perfectly to connect my forehead with the ball, twisting my neck, hoping to see that whoosh at the rear of the net. Instead, I kept looking over my shoulder, trying to catch a glimpse. I knew they would both be in the stands at some point.

Eventually there they were, next to each other, I could see them speaking. Instead of paying attention to the ball I was fixated on my parents' proximity to each other. Setting up for a throw-in, speeding to receive a pass, tripping over the ball as I tried to deke, all I could think was, *Is my mom going to say something?*

Walking across the turf, I could feel it squish under my cleats as I readjusted my soccer bag over my shoulder and squirted water in my mouth. I could see my mom and dad standing close-ish. It took the wind out of me more than the ninety minutes of running did.

They separated some as I approached. My tired legs cringed as I made my way up the large steps. I gave my mom a hug and said good-bye, it was the first of the month, so I was going home to my father's.

"Love you, Mom," I said as I stepped away with my dad.

"Love you, too, hon."

My chest pained, but I tried to hide it. Post soccer was the perfect time to disguise feelings—lower back, knees, burning thighs . . . an abundance of hiding places.

Sinking into the passenger seat of my dad's car, I placed my bag on the floor in front of me, keeping my shoulders and head in a general downward direction.

Maybe she didn't say anything? Maybe they just chatted?

Too much time went by with too little noise, making those "maybes" feel obsolete.

My father drove in silence down Quinpool Road, past Horseshoe Island, along the water, up and around the Armdale rotary. He veered left at the pizza place to Purcells Cove Road. As we approached the turn into our neighborhood, the vehicle did not slow. I caught a glance of my dad, who I am sure knew I was looking, but kept his gaze solidly ahead. His mouth was tight.

We continued for about five minutes, passing St. George's Greek Orthodox Church, the Yacht Club and Deadman's Island, until turning left onto narrow Dingle Road. Surrounded by thick trees and the occasional home, the car wound down to arrive at Sir Sandford Fleming Park, mostly known as "The Dingle."

The bottom of the park sits on the water. My dad turned into the gravel lot, not far from the 132-foot stone tower that was built in the early twentieth century. We'd walked to the top with Linda, Scott, and Ashley a few years prior. Two large bronze lions sit on either side of the entrance, always asking to be climbed on. I remember the tower having more stairs than I would have liked, but the view was worth it, and so was the scoop of Moon Mist after, a delicious ice cream flavor that I only just learned is specific to Nova Scotia.

He parked in the shade and turned off the ignition. It was early evening, there were not many people about, just two other cars in the wide lot. Looking forward, his hands were still on the wheel. I sat silently. He turned to me. His eyes welled up.

"You want to go live at your mom's?"

He started to cry. It sucked the breath from me, I just stared, unsure what to do, unsure what was next.

"Why don't you want to live with us anymore?"

His head dropped. The crying turned into sobbing.

"You love your mother more than me?"

The weeping continued. Shoulders rising and falling. He looked at me, and his sad eyes hit like a rock. I could feel their weight.

"Do you not love me?"

My chest caught fire with panic, my stomach plummeted like a fair ride, leaving a ring in the ears.

He turned back, the bawling did not stop.

I undid my seat belt and clambered over the center console to hug my father. I wrapped my arms around him, rubbing his back as he cried. My body shook, what had I done? Eyes shut as I held tight, I wished I'd said nothing, desperate to take it back.

"I love you. I am sorry. I still want to go back and forth. I'm sorry," I said with a pleading tone.

"Well, are you sure though?" he replied. His shoulders slowly returned to their normal state, as he wiped away tears.

"Yes, I am sure. I want to live with mom and you."

The emotion calming down to sniffles, I sat back down and clicked my seat belt back into place.

"I love you so much," he said as he turned on the car.

The gravel crunched as he reversed.

"I love you, too."

And we drove home.

When we got back it was as if nothing had happened. Just a blip. Alone in the car I was desperately wanted, now here we were, at the dinner table. He cut his food with a dour expression. The silence evaporated my appetite, or was it the guilt? I wanted to disappear.

My father called that night to let my mother know that I had changed my mind. He told her the only reason I wanted to live at my mom's full-time in the first place was because I missed the dog. I assume his frown turned into a gloating smirk, thrilled to update her.

My mother never brought it up. We did not speak of it. I felt too scared to say one more word about it. In the car I had watched my father's heart crack, a wave of emotion I'd never seen, a dismantling. *You did a horrible and hurtful thing,* I'd think. I knew I could never cause him to feel such a way again, or anyone. So I kept going back and forth between households. That seemed to smooth things out.

I can see now how moments like these—between me, my mom, my dad—silently paved the way for my future relationship dynamics. I would throw the feelings aside, worried I'd get in trouble for having them, remaining in situations a lot longer than I should have, hide my truth. Inevitably, this would always lead to more damage and more harm. Like the many ways in which I have been difficult for people—my abrupt shifts, shutting down mixed with the instinct to run, being dishonest because I felt so irrationally frightened.

It is fruitful to dig through the muck.

It was not too long after my thirtieth birthday that I made the decision to stop talking to my father for a while. My ability to suppress my feelings waning. A mental storm, a collision. I'd unconsciously chipped away to reach the bottom. For the first time I was acknowledging my transness out loud, allowing this knowledge to breathe without obstruction, brief moments, sparks, not just grazing it, but holding. This understanding did not stop at my gender. Finally, I was on the verge of disentangling myself from toxic family dynamics, at last able to find the words.

I sent him a short and direct email stating I needed space and wouldn't be able to come home for some time. I had never given myself permission to speak up to him, to own what I'd experienced in that household and its lasting impact. His response was as I expected—not good. He didn't seem capable of taking responsibility for anything I shared.

My father had acknowledged Linda's treatment of me back in my early twenties when I brought it up over coffee. There had been noticeable distance. I was on a rare trip home, and my father and I were in a small, intimate café on Hollis Street in downtown Halifax.

"It feels like you don't miss us, that you never want to see us," my father said.

Looking down at my double Americano, I wasn't sure how to respond. Even when my stepbrother and stepsister's father died, I didn't travel back for the funeral. In therapy, I couldn't explain why, I had no answer. I lay on the floor, crying, my stomach full of nails, a sharp pain, an unknown origin. It felt physically impossible. Understandably, my siblings may have never forgiven me for that.

"I feel so disconnected from you," he followed up.

I had no plan to have the conversation, it just came out.

"Linda was pretty horrible to me when I was growing up and it has affected me and I'm finding it hard to be home and around you," I said.

He wasted no time, agreeing instantly. I was not yet capable of approaching my father about other things. Showing hints of relief, he was able to pin it all on her.

"Why did you not do something if you knew?" I asked.

"I did. Ninety percent of our fights were about you." He echoed the line from my childhood.

I felt a glimmer of hope—the hold that family has over us. But then he told Linda about our conversation, which caused an eruption. She quickly wrote me a long letter, an apology, which was less of an apology and more of an explanation, outlining all of the reasons that caused her hostility. I was a kid. Reasons that ultimately had nothing to do with me.

"You should forgive Linda," my dad said to me forty-eight hours later. "It would be good for you."

I sunk. I had to say it. That's how it felt at least, an obligation. For them, but mostly for him. It's that moment—the body freezes, autopilot, the words ejected for a steady landing. Like writing those birthday cards, a hand not my own. We cried and hugged.

Linda said she was sorry, that she loved me.

"I forgive you," I said. But I didn't, not yet at least.

But by the time I was thirty, my father's means of control faltered. Suddenly, I could see through it, aghast I hadn't before, shedding the reflex to throw my feelings aside, to make myself disappear.

I haven't spoken with my father in five and a half years. When I first sent an email saying I needed space and wouldn't be able to come home for a while, it did not go over well. There have been unpleasant email exchanges from time to time, but that has been the extent of it. Not long ago I suggested we Zoom with a moderator, a family therapist of some sort, but initially he refused, saying he would only meet alone. Eventually, he agreed, but the conversation felt frustratingly similar to our previous interactions, without much resolution.

To be frank, it is hard to imagine a relationship again. Dennis and Linda support those with massive platforms who have attacked and ridiculed me on a global scale. Regardless of everything before, it's painful to think that someone who parented you could support those who deny your very existence.

I will receive enormous waves of hate, not because I made harmful jokes, but because I am trans. It often seems like more people step forward to defend being unkind than they do to support trans people as we deal with an onslaught of cruelty and violence.

When Jordan Peterson was let back on Twitter after he'd made a horrific tweet about me, he posted a video, just his head filling the frame. Staring menacingly into the camera, he said, "We'll see who cancels who." My dad "liked" it. I have no clue what my father thinks of his son at this point, what he says, how he explains my absence. I do know that I am blamed, the one who made the mess, that little skid mark.

The lowest point in my life came after I stopped speaking with my father. The weight of everything I'd grown up with finally hit me, and I was unable to hide. My life has always come in undulating waves, and this low moment was reminiscent of a time when I was nineteen, just as my career was taking off. I wasn't really living anywhere at the time, no home base. Traveling constantly, I was going from one project to the next, press tours, always alone. The weight of loneliness was taking its toll.

In a gesture of kindness I will never forget, a woman I knew from childhood offered to let me crash at her place in Brooklyn. She had been living between Halifax and Fort Greene ever since she started dating the mother of my high school friend. Her relationship with my friend's mom captivated me, in a whole league of their own, no restrictions. I remember so clearly meeting Julia for the first time. I was sixteen, on their bedroom floor, my hoodie pulled over a recently shaved head, curled up in a nest of blankets, ready to sleep over. She walked in the room, and I grinned up at her. Her eyes conveyed tenderness, a presence I could trust. She saw the secret we all knew was in me. I sensed she knew it, and in that knowing I could relax. I always felt comfortable and cared for with her.

Julia suggested that I drop the never fully unpacked luggage off at her Brooklyn loft and create a home, a base, a place to come back to between shoots. Less drifting. The loft had two small bedrooms in the rear, and in the space between, she set up two shoji screens that we purchased in Chinatown, creating a little nook for me. I was in and out, traveling constantly for work, but having that foundation to return to, a queer one, was pivotal.

Julia and I were both extremely early risers, she would make strong and mouthwatering coffee, all fancy like on her stove. We'd hit the streets in the morning, barely past dawn, taking the dogs, Scooby and Dolly, on a looping walk around Fort Greene Park. The relationship evolved. I became closer with Julia than I ever was with my friend from high school. I loved hanging out with her, preferred it in fact. Spending such a significant amount of my life around adults from the age of ten onward, I found myself more comfortable in her presence than that of my peers. I could discuss a bevy of topics that I never would with others, including my crushes and queerness.

Julia became one of my best friends, more like family in fact.

Eventually I moved out, ultimately settling in Los Angeles. Still, when I'd travel to NYC for press, we would spend endless time together in the fancy hotel rooms I was put up in. The Regency, the Mercer, the London, the Mandarin Oriental, the Crosby, the Bowery . . . She was a lifeline to me when I was closeted and continued that role well into my adult life.

When I stopped speaking to my father, I spiraled. I was on the brink, my mental health plummeting. I didn't want to be in this world anymore. I didn't know how to be. I called Julia from Los

Angeles and asked if she could come be with me, knowing what would happen if I was left alone. My call shocked her—I so rarely asked for help. She dropped everything, took a week off work, and flew to LA.

While Julia was in town we sat among cozy blankets on my living room floor, a protective nest like I'd been burrowed in the first time we met. She helped me nourish my body, she made me laugh. I blabbered away about the same shit on repeat and she listened. It didn't matter how raw, sad, or enraged I was, Julia let me feel.

In a world where queerness all too often alienates us from blood, I am grateful to Julia, and the family I have chosen. Without them, I wouldn't be here.

26

MASK

——

"Pardon, monsieur," a man said to me after his five- or six-year-old child came barreling down the hill on a small blue scooter, coming close to hitting my dog, Mo.

The kid sped by during that first spring of the pandemic in New York City. Empty streets, space, silence minus the sirens and the occasional speaker pumping tunes from a passing bike. I was wearing a mask, I can't remember if the man and his child were. There was a chill in the air, the wind from the river typically stung the face, but the mask proved helpful. I wore jeans and my flannel-lined black Carhartt jacket with my hooded sweatshirt poking out. A hat, always a hat, my beanie snug under the hood.

Mo and I were walking up from the path that runs along the Hudson River to the middle level of Riverside Park on the Upper West Side. The park is one of my favorite places in New York City. It has three levels and runs from 72nd Street to 158th Street. The path along the river has green areas, playgrounds, a tiny marina called the West 79th Street Boat Basin. A compact old forest-green boat floated quietly while I was playing "Which would be your boat?"—a highly complicated game in which you say which boat would be yours. I decided on that little guy. The promenade, the middle tier just above, has a design similar to parks in Paris, long, wide paths, tree branches above, curling to meet. Old streetlamps frame the cement, standing proud, while exuding romance. Stunning cliffs and stone walls, festooned with vines and moss, reach from the promenade to the top tier, which runs along Riverside Drive. Can parks be emotional? Feels that way, its beauty is haunting. I read Riverside Park inspired Edgar Allan Poe to write "The Raven." Makes sense.

"That's okay," I responded, Mo caught off guard by the sudden tug. Stepping away, I could hear the father speaking to his child in French, not harsh but firm. Again I heard *monsieur*.

A smile formed under my mask. This had been occurring frequently.

"Yo, man."

"Bro."

"Sir."

It was not until I spoke that they would clock me with embarrassment—

"Oh, sorry, miss."

"Sorry, ma'am."

I used to interrogate my shadow as I made my way about the city. It lived on the sidewalk, flat and underfoot, a quiet moment between me and the sun. I saw a boy, it was a boy, his body, his walk, the profile with the ball cap. The spot on the ground felt more real than me and dodged my attempts to squash it.

Storefront windows and I had forever been in a contentious relationship. Unlike the shadow, I could see my face, my torso in a T-shirt. The fall and winter were not *as* bad, but the summer led to cranks in the neck. Too hot for layers, I'd compulsively turn to look, checking and readjusting. Tugging down my oversize white T, I'd remind myself to get tighter sports bras. *Maybe that would help.*

During the beginning of the pandemic, my mask collaborated with my early spring wardrobe to alter my reflection in the window. Like my shadow, I saw the boy. Unlike the shadow, the boy looked back at me.

A thrilling vibration throughout my body I was not anticipating. It was jarring in a good way—a rush.

What the actual fuck?! My reflection never gives me "a rush."

Peeking at the boy stomping parallel to me, matching my mannerisms, my pace. I was baffled and also totally not. It didn't get old, every day when I walked Mo I'd find him, a reprieve. Hope?

The soles of my feet pressed firm, confident and grounded. Less of that floating, a more cohesive bond with gravity. It was gratifying seeing myself, which almost never happened. There was a spark, a seed, something getting stirred up. My body leaned in, knowing not to stop there, sensing it before my mind did. This flesh vessel, always vastly smarter than me, if only I'd managed to listen. A path had formed out of the blue, luring instinct. A few knocks on the back of the closet, a portal to a new world, a fresh reality in which I did not have to abandon myself.

I was not being recognized at all. Not even the subtle double-takes. I'm not R. Patz by any means, but this was like stepping into another dimension. And regardless of how much you are stopped or asked for a photo, people look. People "sneak" a picture on the train or at restaurants, not realizing I can usually tell—in some strange way it is quite endearing. I do not mind taking pictures with people at all. People are usually friendly and kind, not forceful. It is only if someone touches me without my consent or calls me by my old name that I become less warm. Boundaries are important, and learning to not feel guilty about setting them is crucial. It took me long enough to learn that.

I wandered around the city in my own newfangled universe. I could just be me, at ease, nothing projected by strangers. And for the first time since age ten, I was having people refer to me as a dude. I tried to not talk much, offering some barely audible grunts to prolong the moments. My voice at ten did not let the cat out of the bag, but at thirty-three it definitely did.

All I knew was something became unglued and now I could let the crack grow. There was no work to run off to, no girl that I had to play. Season three of *The Umbrella Academy* would not start filming until late fall, the earliest. This was my longest period of not working in . . . I don't remember, and arguably my first proper break in years. My marriage was crumbling, we were living separately, and days were not *as* wrapped up in drama and distraction and suppression. There was time to sit, a moment to think. All that space initially amplified the discomfort. I had spent years and years figuring out all the tricks to avoid my feelings, to exit my body, numb it out. But now, something was simmering, preparing to bubble over, I could feel it. Outside in my layers and concealed face I was solid, taking in optimistic saunters. Inside was different. Taking off my mask, my jacket, I'd be snapped out of my reverie. Changing my clothes felt impossible, I was barely showering, the thought of removing and putting on my sports bra made me cringe. Those seeds of hope, the whispers of a better future, evaporated the moment I entered my apartment. The contrast between exterior and interior heightened my unease, a graph with a climbing linear line that soon was bound to plummet. I was nearing that edge again, and no matter how challenging, how destabilizing— I knew I needed to sink in, to not be afraid, to love myself.

In therapy, I continued opening up about my relationship to gender. I was slowly developing the skill to speak the words I needed to without an endless surge of sobs. Instead of being completely thrown off track, I was able to address the torment, to zoom out, to question why it had to be so agonizing. How come I could not just breathe and explore? Why did it need to come with a truckload of shame?

Not living with Emma did let some of my anxiety dissipate. A fixation and focus only for their feelings had been wearing me thin. I felt that Emma's emotions always took precedence over mine. This, I am certain, was purposeful on my part. The avoidance, the running, the numbing, the disassociating—all of my nifty tactics at their best. Harmful for me and harmful for them. And ultimately, it had nothing to do with Emma.

As the summer rolled in, I was back to oversize T-shirts, the required tugging and looking. The shop windows did not put a pep in my step, no longer were people referring to me as my correct gender. I first started to properly contemplate top surgery during this time. Realistically it had been on my mind for years. Reaching out to surgeons was the first step. I made an appointment for a consultation, but I did not end up going. I couldn't specifically say why—whether it was fear or circumstance.

I picked up Marin, my costar from *The Umbrella Academy,* one morning at her place in Chelsea, and we drove out to Coney Island. Masks on, windows down, we caught up. We hadn't seen each other in a little while. Marin played Sissy, the woman my character falls in love with in the 1960s in Texas in the second season. Collaborating with Marin was one of the best experiences I have ever had working with another actor. She's brilliant, generous, and so fucking in it, deep and present in a way that is rare. Basically, I had been talking about my gender and discomfort with Marin since we met. We instantly became friends. The first time we spoke on the phone before meeting each other, we talked for over two hours. It was as if we had known each other for years. The second season of *Umbrella* was a mixed bag for me. On one hand the character was more masculine, the clothes I far preferred to the previous season, but in the mirror I was still there. It was as if I expected the wardrobe to magically change me and it did, for a split second, but my reflection promptly corrected my thinking. My face, my hair, I wanted to rip it off and rip it out.

Marin was a rock for me during this period. I was struggling and did not know how to communicate it. She helped me, supported me, encouraged me to take time and focus on my well-being, to give myself space. As I crept closer to my truth, unconscious shame reared its head, bullying me to shut it down. It was hard to exist without diversion. Being alone I felt adrift. I mostly sat on the floor and smoked way too much weed, for some reason a couch wasn't working for me. Stop too long, get too comfortable, and you'll find the answer you do not want, but the answer you need. My brain was doing everything to get around it, for it to not be the case, it was just too fucking much to contemplate. An actor, an established career, people hate trans people . . . etc.

The hollow sound of the boardwalk emerged from each step. What is it about a boardwalk? It was hot, early July. The sun peered through the clouds, heavenly beams shot down into the ocean. Most things were boarded up, the amusement park silent, ghostly. Coney Island in the summer is usually overrun with people, but the pandemic had put a stop to that. Still, kids screamed and played in the water. Fathers carried burgers and fries. It was cinematic, time slowed. Men we passed stared at Marin for too long, and it made me angry.

I forgot where we parked so it was a journey to find the car, the stress of the day simmering. When we finally found it, I burst into tears, sobbing.

I turned to Marin. "Do you think I'm trans?"

"Um, it is hard for me to answer that, but between all the things you have shared with me and seeing how it has not let up and how painful it is for you, yes, perhaps. I think you are on the right track and I know this is hard, but you are not alone, you will get through this."

Exhale.

My marriage had properly ended, personally not legally, that June.

I decided to give up the apartment we had been renting. One of my closest friends had an empty cabin in the middle of the woods in Nova Scotia and said I could stay there. I had not seen my mother in ages, so heading up seemed like the smartest idea. Leaving the United States felt nothing like before. The border was shut, I was able to go because I am a citizen, and while I packed up the car, tears started streaming. The beginning of the pandemic was full of unknowns, an unprecedented event we were living through and still are. I did not know when I would see my friends again.

Mo in his booster seat and me in the driver's seat, we were ready for our journey. The drive in and out of the city I always find mildly terrifying. But then you get to Connecticut and you are surrounded by trees upon trees. The coast of Maine let my nervous system take a break, rugged with salty air, the smell of the ocean rushing by the open window, reminding me of home, almost there. I spent the night in Bangor to split the thirteen-to-fourteen-hour drive into two days. The hotel was desolate, but immaculately clean. Mo and I crashed early and were on the road by 6:00 A.M.

Emma got rid of their place in the city, too, and made their way up to Montreal. We were barely communicating, I'm not sure where Emma was staying exactly. The quarantine for new arrivals in Nova Scotia was two weeks. My mom and her friends were kind enough to put food in the cabin for me. On top of dropping off groceries, they made me homemade soup and cookies.

The cabin is connected to a dirt road by an unpaved driveway. Arriving there is like entering a living fairy tale. Yellow birches, maples, and pine trees line the road. There is a small orchard that has not been touched in decades. Left free to grow, pears and apples scatter the ground. Deer paths wind through the tall grass. Snakes wriggle all over the property, nothing poisonous. There are a few that live in the greenhouse, and I like to say hi when I go over to water the plants—tomatoes, squash, peppers, kale, and more.

The cabin had been recently built. Other than a bed and a couple deck chairs, there was no furniture. For press, my computer sat on a blue Coleman cooler with a ring light right behind. The internet was so weak that the Netflix publicity team was understandably stressed, but it ended up being fine. I eventually added an old red chrome dining table. I had bought it when I was twenty and rented my first apartment in Halifax, down by the train station on the corner of South and Barrington. I'd given it to Nikki, who didn't need it anymore. We'd become close again, and she returned it to me, perfect timing.

The two weeks of isolation flew by, I had a whole whack of press for the second season of *The Umbrella Academy.* I was grateful to be in the middle of the woods, the silence and darkness allowing my body to crash. Interviews and a lot of sleeping essentially. Mo was happy as a clam. He seemed in shock the first few days we were there, he would just sit on the patio and stare out at the woods, his ears twitching and head pivoting toward the sounds of ravens and squirrels and deer clomping through the brush. As far as I know he had never been in nature like that. He is very small, seven pounds, so I have to keep an eye on him. I wish I could let him take off through the forest, but there are coyotes and foxes that could eat him up, and hawks, eagles, and ravens that could scoop him up. I have never had a connection with a dog like I have with Mo. Dogs I have had in the past, I loved them dearly, but Mo is different. We are attached at the hip, I am obsessed, so much it hurts. Mo is an infinitely joyous little being who exudes love every minute of the day. Having Mo gave me a lot—routine, responsibility, walking, but primarily he expanded my heart. The care I feel is bottomless, a lesson learned from Mo. Without words he helped me, I began to offer some of that care for myself and to make the commitment to accept it.

When the press ended, I was left with no distractions. I hung out with Mo, I read, hiked a lot. I enjoyed doing chores, stacking wood, sheet mulching, taking care of the greenhouse. A peacefulness washed over me, a focus so pure. This was in direct contrast with the conflict in my body, the strain on my brain was burning me out, clouding everything. I reverted to not changing my clothes, not showering, sleeping in them, getting up in them. Changing socks and underwear was possible, but my shirt, nope.

Nikki came to visit for a weekend, and we went to Blue Sea Beach, a thirty-minute-or-less drive from the cabin. Nikki is always prepared for the beach in the summer, her Prius trunk contained an umbrella, beach chairs, a blanket—so smart. "Canada's Ocean Playground" has a bounty of spectacular beaches. We parked and lugged everything to the beach that stretched on for an entire mile. We set up our zone, it wasn't that busy. Nikki wore her one-piece swimsuit, and I wore boxers and a sports bra because I did not own a bathing suit, and hadn't for a long time.

We took off our shirts and I looked down. My breasts were smooshed inside my tight Nike sports bra. I got it while making the first season of *Umbrella Academy*. I walked into the first wardrobe fitting and said, "I have to wear sports bras, because I need my chest to be pressed down." I had not been that forthcoming about physical needs and costume in a long, long time, but I was working with people who I felt safe with and could communicate to without feeling judged or demeaned.

Nikki and I lathered each other up with sunscreen. She looked confident in her body, lounging in the sun. I had a hard time relaxing. Always. Shifting from one side to the other, sneaking a quick glance at my boobs and my stomach. I had always worked hard on my core, and I wished its flatness would extend up the remainder of my torso. We snacked on chips and pop as the sun lotion settled. The heat was fierce, I was grateful for the umbrella and Nikki's beach preparedness.

Fired up and ready for a dip, I stood and walked toward the surf. Breaking into a run, my feet hit the ocean, splashing the surprisingly warm water with every step. The Northumberland Strait is said to have the warmest ocean temperatures north of Virginia because of how shallow it is, ranging in depth between seventeen and sixty-eight meters. Separating Nova Scotia and Prince Edward Island, the sunsets are always astounding. I dove into the salt water, it had been ages since I was in the ocean. I surfed for a couple years in Los Angeles, my ex Samantha and I went almost every day when we were together. I do miss it, frightening but soothing all the same, it is easy to see how people become addicted. The rush, the connection, you look at the ocean in an entirely new way.

I swam farther out, warm but still refreshing. My eyes stung, and I made a mental note that goggles would be a part of the beach collection in my trunk. I resurfaced, my ponytail soaked and dripping down my back. My body went frigid, not due to the cold, but because I caught a glimpse again. It wrenched me out of the present. My head involuntarily tilted down, chin to my neck, as it did throughout the day every day. My insides tightened, my brow furrowed, puzzled by a body that did not compute. An incorrect calculation that I did not have the answer to. It was exhausting and only getting worse. *How will I do this forever?*

Nikki went for a swim shortly after me. I dried myself with a towel, avoiding my chest. The blanket sat in the shade. I lay on my stomach, my boobs compressed, taunting me, jogging my memory, demanding I be reminded. I closed my eyes, the sound of the waves pacified me, and I fell asleep.

Nikki and I napped on the beach together, when we woke up it was time to go. I threw on a T-shirt and we gathered our things. Walking back to the car, I looked around at the people enjoying themselves. Kids and their sandcastles. Two guys threw a football back and forth, swim shorts and no shirts. The ball flew with a perfect spin. A woman with a half tent organized snacks, children ran up for juice boxes and ketchup chips. My brain was as hot as the sand.

How do people do it? How do they shut off the noise? And I don't mean "happy," they may not be happy, but they seem to be able to exist at least.

People existed with a fluidity that I wished to possess. Motion entwined with the present and an engagement with life that I had lost a long time ago. I needed my routine, I needed specific food. Change or disruption threw me off, which was unacceptable due to my need for control. All I could do was cling. Every day I hung on tight, bound up. A blockage of sorts. I would need to drain the wound.

In the evening we sat around a bonfire. We sat close, sharing a joint, and leaned back to stare at the stars. I looked toward the orchard, it glittered with slithers of moonlight. The darkness behind the trees made me feel useless, no stars would ever guide me to safety, I could not speak their language.

Nikki and I could be apart for years but within moments of reuniting sync up all over again. As I write this, I will be driving up to Nova Scotia next week. The trip will be my first time to Halifax since sharing the whole trans thing with the world. My grip less tight, my mind relaxed, finally the space to hold it all. I am eager to be with Nikki. I want to hug her, look her in the eyes, to show her who I have become, to show her that I made it. It is July right now, so I am certain the beach trunk will come to good use, and this time, no ponytail and no fucking sports bra. Just there with an old friend to soak life in.

After Nikki left, I was alone in the woods again, which I love. I wasn't sure if I could be someone who lived in a cabin by themselves in the middle of the forest for months, but turns out, I very much am and it may be necessary in order for me to get to the bottom of my own brain. I had to be isolated, I had to not be something to someone or someone to something. I'd exhausted myself, trying with all of me to figure out what was wrong, running from one place to the next, fooling myself into thinking I could find it. But the answer was in the silence, the answer would only come when I chose to listen.

27

PORTAL

———

When I was in the cabin, I found myself able to connect with creativity again. That muscle I was accustomed to using in front of a camera suddenly held untold possibilities. I started writing a screenplay with an old friend, Beatrice Brown.

We'd met when I was sixteen. The day after wrapping a film in Shelburne, Nova Scotia, I flew across the Atlantic. I had landed the lead in a film called *Mouth to Mouth,* which would be shot in the UK, Germany, and Portugal. It was my first time in London, and in Europe in general. I was playing Sherry, a sixteen-year-old runaway who joins a radical collective in Camden Town called SPARK and follows them to their commune on the outskirts of Lisbon. As typically happens in the movies, things go awry, and Sherry must do whatever she can to get away from the controlling and abusive leader before it is too late.

Bea was cast as Nancy, a teenager who grew up in squats, just as Bea had. The character was in part based on Bea, actually, who had often moved around Europe in a small RV, squatting on vacant land and abandoned industrial parks. There was a lot of ketamine, a lot of illegal raves, and a lot of punk music. Bea had a band called

Beastellabeast with Stella Nova (aka Stella New), the guitar legend who played with the Rich Kids, Iggy Pop, and Generation X. You do not meet many people in your life like Bea, if any. She is not afraid of people's silly perceptions and if she is, fuck it, she still takes life head-on.

That first night in London, Bea took me around various squats in Dalston. I'd never been to a squat before. We visited pals of Bea's at one place where the floor and walls were all gray-and-white concrete with very little light. Bare mattresses, sleeping bags, and blankets were scattered around the room. As we were leaving, a dude who appeared a touch strung out threw lightbulbs at us. They smashed on the pavement as we briskly walked down the road. I worried about dogs' paws.

"This is called Murder Mile," Bea said as one of her nipples peeked through a hole in her torn white-and-green vintage dress.

The next squat had a very different vibe, practically posh. An old town house with a large backyard. A place with character, light coming through half-repaired cracked windows. It was packed with people, some watching a projected film, others dancing to music and milling about. Someone always offering you something.

I had my first sex scene on the set of *Mouth to Mouth*. It was with Eric Thal, an actor double my age who played the group's leader. This was not a romantic, intimate scene, but coercive and abusive. It took place in a vineyard in Portugal. Outside, behind the main house, chickens pecked about. I had a half-shaved head and wore a tattered jean vest covered in black marker drawings. Eric, shirtless with broad shoulders and strong torso, towered above me. His buzzed hair left his face exposed and full. He never spoke much to me or anyone, which is of course fine, no one is required to be social. I did wonder if he was Method though, purposefully keeping himself separate.

It was a brutal scene to shoot. I was nearly naked, cold back pressed into the hard ground, and Eric, for whatever reason, kept shouting inches from my face. He'd get up, walk away, yell incoherently, and then return on top. No one seemed to mind but me. After the final take of the final shot, the director sat next to me on the cobblestones and burst into tears. I comforted her.

Beatrice and I speak of this period as adults, reflecting on our behavior, their behavior. What seemed clear and pure then is murky now. But I can hold that and also know this was one of the most important times in my life.

Sitting in the back of a pickup truck, driving through the Portuguese countryside, ponytail blowing in the wind, Bob Dylan blaring out of the stereo, speeding by the *Quercus suber* trees, the trees that produce cork and make up over a quarter of the country's forests—they are everywhere. Their thick and bumpy bark is extracted and shipped all over the world. Underneath, a dark reddish trunk revealed. The color reminded me of the red soil on Prince Edward Island. They stand sixty-five-feet tall, branches contorted, climbing up to the sky and showing off their coriaceous leaves, which do not fall. Such resilience, growing their skin back again and again. I stared at them in awe, lining the road, never ending. I loved their shape, their pride, the beauty of imperfection. This is one of the moments I breathed in so hard as to never forget.

Both feelings can exist, making up the whole, a fullness that I would not trade, something I try to remind myself when old sentiments turn up.

Bea and I had always spoken about collaborating on a creative project, and now—she in Oxford, me in the cabin with Mo—we had the time, we found routine, discipline, and pushed when we were stuck. It was fun, I found myself stretching my imagination in different ways. I tacked colored note cards on a bulletin board in the cabin, I spent hours talking with Bea, writing. Thinking.

We were shocked how easy it was for us previously to have gotten distracted, to jump our lives over to something else, for someone else. To get wrapped up in an unhealthy relationship and have that become the endless, the only, part of our conversations. Something to distract, to get in the way. For me, I was utterly flummoxed that my brain had the space, that I could sit long enough with any of it. A mind unclouded lets the truth look through. I could sense it over my shoulder, but I was still too frightened to turn.

I had canceled that initial consultation with the surgeon in New York City and never rescheduled. I found myself doing what I could to avoid the conversation, and with any friend who had known, I shut it down. Losing myself in tumultuous spirals that only extended to my therapist, and some not even to her.

I just need to learn to be comfortable.
I am being too extreme.
I just need tighter sports bras.
You can't, you're an actor.
Suck it up.
Suck it up.
Suck it up.

Was I going to U-turn again? Or perhaps another would bring me home, return me to when I almost reached it, a last-minute stumble, a jump for the train.

I sat in a small blue, green, and white lawn chair on the front porch, a spot I had unofficially made mine. It's where I probably spent most of my time there. And where I am sitting again as I write this, looking out the same window. The wild plants and grass are much higher, the top rising a foot or so above the sill. A wall of trees stands at the bottom of the hilled yard. The tips of their bright summer leaves sway in front of the high noon blue, with stoic evergreens intermixed throughout.

My mind kept returning to this question, whenever I saw anyone who knew me—really knew me—so I asked Bea: "When was the first time I spoke to you about potentially being trans?"

I was surprised at how long ago it was. Right before my twenty-ninth birthday:

"The first time was back when I lived in Stroud. After a long silence you asked me if I thought you were trans, there was like a hot tsunami of emotion coming from you, and time slowed down and everything expanded, and it felt like a relief. It was the conversation that hid behind our growing up together, back when we had no words, or at least, I didn't, just a sensation, and when the words began to flow, it was this sweet juxtaposition of something hard to be said at first, but also so easy and light, this sense of a world finding its breath, one that resonated with your essential life force."

I can state unequivocally that I would not be here without Bea.

Fuck, I've made so many U-turns it seems the dizziness has affected my memory. Receiving this from Bea prompted flashbacks. Friends I had asked, friends I had told. And again and again, I pushed it down, down, and down. I moved on to the next role, the next photo shoot, the next relationship, the next airport, the next tighter sports bra. *I just have to deal.*

The blue, green, and white lawn chair squeaked whenever I moved. In the middle of the night, the tiniest movement could startle a buck that unknown to me was standing in the darkness. The panicked bolt made Mo go off, the excellent guard dog he is.

My brain would not stop. I was writing in the day, reading, going on long hikes by myself that I should not have been going on by myself. When the evening hit, the dark sky reached to the forest floor, complete silence other than a far-off truck making its way down a distant road. In that stillness, it would come tumbling down, but there was nothing left to say, nothing left to do. I felt trapped, unable to take off my clothes, sleeping with my shoes on. The candlelight flickered on the window, making my reflection barely visible. I looked down to my hand and clenched it. The words were always the same, I just needed to shut up.

Hard and sharp, I struck myself with my knuckles. Surprised at my temerity, I glanced back down at my fist. Inspecting it, I looked at both sides and then, WHAM! Again. And again. Harder. Sharper. I pummeled my face, pounding next to my right eye. Some other force working to knock it out.

Bruises materialized. I'd be seeing people in a couple days, friends who were coming up to stay briefly at another cabin nearby. I had to surmise a way of explaining it, or a way of hiding it.

Did I trip and fall? Hit the side of the table?

That seemed made up. I iced it on and off, obsessively checking the mirror.

Maybe I dropped my phone on my face while lying on my back?

The bruise was way too big for that.

Maybe you need to just tell someone?

Nope, I wasn't going to do that. I attempted to cover the shiner with foundation. Dabbing it with my finger, trying different strategies. It worked somewhat.

My face hurt, but the pain came mostly from shame and guilt. I felt awful about what I had done to my body, about covering up for my self-abusive self. Sleeping in my shoes was one thing, battering my face was different, a breaking point. And there it was, that edge again. A body smarter than me.

A few days later, back in my favorite chair, I watched the trees as gusts of wind passed through like clockwork. The movement of the branches interrupted the late afternoon sun, the beams pierced through and waltzed effortlessly with the motion. The marks left by my fist had partially faded, the sting as well. *Discreet Music* by Brian Eno spun on the record player.

I had a flashback to the feeling on the beach with Nikki. My chest, the staring down, wanting more pressure but despising the reminder. There was always a reminder. Unable to shower, remove my hoodie, eat without anxiety, or eat at all. Sadness came over me, a grief and anger, livid that I could not just *be.* Exhausted by the distress, a brain that was about to crack, unsure if I was able to cope.

And then something happened.

You don't have to feel this way.

That voice.

I don't have to feel this way?

That fucking voice.

You don't have to feel this way.

I don't have to feel this way.

This was not miracle water that sprang out of nowhere. This was a long-ass journey. However, this moment was indeed that simple, as it should be—deciding to love yourself. There had been multiple forks in the road, and more than once I had taken the wrong path, or not, depends on how you look at it I guess. It is painful the unraveling, but it leads you to you.

There it finally was, a portal. It was time to step through.

28

NO WORDS

———

Filming for the third season of *The Umbrella Academy* was due to commence in January. If I wasn't able to get the surgery within three months, it would mean waiting another year. The space for doubt was gone, there was no more room for second-guessing. I was thirty-three. From the moment I decided, I had not a single second thought, no little whisper telling me to throw the shift into reverse. I was able to get a consultation scheduled for a month later, they did not think the timing was possible for the operation.

Then, a cancellation. My initial conversation with the surgeon was pulled up by two weeks and a slot for the procedure was now available on November 17, in the nick of time. I thought my Zoom with the doctor would be emotional and overwhelming, it could not have been more chill. Nothing but smiles. I felt listened to, I felt safe. My whole body took a deep breath.

This is a complicated matter to write about, because some people who are reading this have to wait years and years to finally have their surgery, or will never have access to gender-affirming care. I can imagine anyone would feel angry, resentful, and roiled by my privilege, what it allows me. Time during a pandemic to not work and self-reflect. I am not from a place where it is illegal. I was able to go to a private clinic and pay the approximately twelve thousand dollars. I had a place to stay. A friend who had the energy to care for me. Food to eat as I recovered. A job right around the corner, one where I could be me. I didn't have to depend on a health-care system that would leave me waiting potentially for years.

Even though I am extremely lucky, this narrative where trans people have to feel *lucky* for these crumbs—that we fought hard for, and still fight for—is perverse and manipulative. Here is the thing—I almost did not make it, the now I finally have I did not see, and all I knew was permanent emptiness, a mystery I would never solve. Incessant, without language, a depth of despair. Shameful, with all that I had—what dreams are made of. I did nothing but sink, dread blanketing me. I couldn't see what was in front of me. I should not have to grovel with gratitude. Am I grateful? Fuck, yeah! But everyone should have access to gender-affirming and lifesaving health care. It just should be.

I left the cabin at 6:00 A.M. on November 12. Car all packed, Mo in his booster seat, a cooler with pop and PB&J, a full tank of gas, prepared for the two-day drive to Toronto. I didn't have much cargo, considering I would be in Ontario for ten months. When I originally drove to Nova Scotia from Manhattan I was not expecting to be gone for such a long period. I assumed Covid would calm down and the borders would reopen by the end of summer. Nope, that was just the beginning.

The air was cool, the sky just before light, mist disappeared as I wove through Wentworth toward Amherst. Sun up, clouds rolled in, a mix of clear and rain. Right when I crossed the border into New Brunswick a massive double rainbow filled the sky. Triumphant. I waved. I planned on splitting the sixteen-or-so-hour drive evenly into two days, but as I drove on November 12, my whole being buzzed. Without music, without a podcast, without a phone chat, I flew by where I was set to spend the night, no part of me ready to slow down. It was 6:00 p.m. in Quebec when I pulled up to a hotel in Old Montreal, a thirteen-hour day in the car. Mo and I went for a tiny stroll, never having seen Montreal this empty and quiet. Tomorrow morning's drive would only be five hours. The cobblestones felt nice under my boots.

Bloodwork and an EKG were required before the procedure. I walked east along Queen Street to LifeLabs, with each brisk step I grew closer. The day of my surgery, November 17, I went to the clinic alone, you were not able to bring a companion due to Covid. Mark dropped me off. Oddly, I was not nervous, all I wanted was the time to move, that bright light above while the ceiling and I grow apart. I was the second surgery of the day, one o'clock. You could not eat or drink anything, including water, before, which felt fine, because my stomach was interested in nothing. I waited in a small room with a bed, TV, and side table with a peaceful lamp. The nurse came in to take my vitals and talk over everything. The morning surgery was running over, so it would most likely be a while. I curled up in the bed, no TV, no book, no music, and I just lay there for three hours until it was time. Like the moment before I came out, holding myself.

On the table. Light above. Mouth covered. Down, down, down.

Mark picked me up after the three-or-so-hour procedure. He took a photo of me when he first walked in the room. I lay there, partially propped up, high as fuck, wearing a black compression vest, my nipples just removed and slapped back on. The smile on my face, in my eyes, the degree of contentment glowing off me, phew.

Mark drove me home from the clinic in Yorkville to where we were staying near Queen and Bathurst. My friend Marin was filming a different show in Toronto, but she would be back in New York for that month, so she offered her place. We made a spot for me on a daybed in the cozy living room with low ceilings. Mark had the bedroom upstairs with a wall of windows looking out onto a beautiful wooden terrace that was often occupied by raccoons.

The recovery felt appropriate, considering the operation. Those first couple days, meds a-rockin', emotion seeped out like my blood in the dangling drains. Poor Mark contended with bursts of grief and anger, at all the time lost, at all the self-hate, at all that could have been. He'd sit with me, listen to me, rub my back, be patient with me. He monitored my medication and measured the drained blood, which dripped through two tubes that came from a tiny hole under each armpit. At the bottom hung little partially red, translucent orbs on either side of my waist.

I was grateful for painkillers and *Shark Tank* and *Guy's Grocery Games*. Mark could be on *Triple G* or *Chopped,* I do believe. Something delicious was always brewing, from dal to apple crisp like nothing. No recipes and always delicious.

Mark stayed with me for a week and a half. A couple days post-op I had my wits about me again. After eating a meal, Mark started fiddling with the Omnichord he had brought, a synth instrument originally developed in 1981. Not very big, it can rest in your lap. With it you have everything from drums to guitar to organ, a little electric world to uncover. Melodies simmered with the rice, beats worked themselves out on the table, the crunch of a half-full popcorn bag offered an interesting sound. Finding the words and the flow, the tone and heart, we set up a recording zone in the compact spare room. Mark brought a 4-track and a microphone, and we started to put the songs together. We huddled, crouched on the carpet, listening back, recording again, lyrics scribbled, changing words, laughing and surprising ourselves, completely lost in creation, in each other, the moment, like being kids again. How lucky that we will always have those songs. How lucky am I for Mark, my love.

This was the most time we'd spent together since backpacking through Eastern Europe. Long, meandering journeys leading us back to the frigid winter in Queen West, Toronto, thirteen years after *Juno*'s premiere. He was my guest at that Toronto International Film Festival. I'll never forget the look on his face when he saw me as hair and makeup did their final touches. His eyes were big, an expression like a stomach drop, he looked on with noticeable concern. I had the urge to take him aside, to explain, but what was there to say?

And after this, there was a drift. We no longer lived in the same city and I progressively disappeared as I tucked myself away. I didn't want to see that expression on his face, I didn't want to be reminded, I already knew. It all felt choiceless. And we never really did talk about it, I felt embarrassed, ashamed, betraying myself felt like betraying him, too.

He knew it wasn't me then. Now, he knew it was.

A couple days after my surgery, we drove to High Park, one of our old haunts as teens. Overestimating my abilities, I grew weak as we were nearing the end of our stroll. Deep breaths, I took my time, not wanting to admit I might not make it. Walking up a hill, I winced. Closing my eyes, I felt Mark hold my hand, squeezing it tight, and we made our way home.

By two weeks I was up and back at it (somewhat). I just would not be able to lift anything over five pounds for the next couple months. I was alone, and changing my nipple bandages on my own was an adjustment. The shock of seeing them, bruised and un-recognizable, tiny bubbles of blood, every time thinking I'd done something wrong and every time learning I had not. The prospect of taking off the compression vest for good, to have my chest out, forward, unconfined . . . wordless, leaning into the mystical. But this was not my imagination. This was finally it. I had to block it out and just wait for the time to tick or it barely fucking ticked. A few more weeks.

The most painful point for me was having the drains removed. Massive needle after massive needle to freeze around the tiny holes under my pits. The nurse stood beside me, speaking calmly as I tried to let go, to embrace the hurt. When both sides were frozen the surgeon was set to remove the tubes. The nurse counted down from three . . . two . . . one, the doctor pulled, it wiggled under my skin, an angry worm forced out from my insides.

I purchased too many button-down shirts online. Typically too big, but some work out. Putting on each, I looked at my profile in the mirror, huge grin, running my hand from my neck to my abdomen. A mini fashion show, a montage sequence gone on way too long. My phone filled up with pictures of my smooth chest, the new angles, that *smile*. It healed well, as planned, my left side a few days behind the right.

And when the vest was gone and the nipple bandages done . . . well, I have no words for that.

As a trans person and a public one, the sensation is that I'm always pleading for people to believe me, which I imagine most trans people relate to. Tired of the wink and nod. When I came out in 2014, the vast majority of people believed me, they did not ask for proof. But the hate and backlash I received were nothing compared to now. Not even close. I was not nervous to tell anyone in my close circle when I came out as gay, but disclosing this new information felt different. I do wonder what some friends say behind my back, what they really think when they look at me.

I am sick of the creepy focus on my body and compulsion to infantilize (which I have always experienced, but nothing like this). And it isn't just people online, or on the street, or strangers at a party, but good acquaintances and friends.

"You look adorable," a pal said at an awards show after-party. Someone who is a Pulitzer Prize–winning progressive force. You're feeling dashing AF, literally for the first time at an event, and then a friend has to roll in with that. Fuck you, "adorable."

"Wow, one of my best friends is trans?!" a bosom buddy said in response to me being me.

"I guess that is just something you don't make a comment about," one of my dearest friends said on the heels of a long pause after I shared my decision to get top surgery, one of the first people I told. She most certainly made "a comment" without "making a comment" and proceeded to make more, offering her opinion un-prompted. I couldn't talk to her for a long time.

"My friend asked if you're going to get the other surgery . . ."

"I was surprised to hear your voice, but I will get used to it."

Or the classic: "This won't give you all the answers, you know that, right?"

Of course. Nothing ever could.

Friends making quips about my facial hair growing in. Jokes about what name I should have chosen. A year and a half later and the pronouns are still just too much for some. I am patient, we all are endlessly learning and I've made the same mistakes, but sometimes patience wears thin. I know these instances and remarks may seem tiny, but when your existence is constantly debated and denied, it sucks you dry. Sprawled out, bare, I crave gentleness.

The truth is, in many ways, my narrative is still unfolding. I have been on testosterone for over a year now. Every Friday I wake up excited yet content, a new sense of calm in my life. I inject myself with forty milligrams of T, I'm changing, I'm growing, it's all just beginning.

Let me just exist with you, happier than ever.

29

PEACHES

———

Mark and I arrived at the Opera House on Queen Street East *early* early. I have never lined up that far in advance for anything and been among the first few in line. We stood freezing in the Toronto winter. Peaches was playing. It was her tour after the release of her second record, *Fatherfucker.* I used to dance like a fatherfucker to it. Shirt off, sports bra tight, blinds down.

The moment we got in, we jogged to the stage, pressing our bodies against it. I waited irritably through the opener. They were good, but the time between them finishing and Peaches emerging crawled. The place continued to fill, lights of purple and red. A sold-out show. And tons and tons of queer people. Arguably the queerest space I had been in at that point in my life.

The Stranglers' song "Peaches" came on, the lights lowered, signaling that she was about to start.

Walking on the beaches, looking at the peaches

The song is only slightly over four minutes, but it felt a whole lot longer, looking it up for this, I'd anticipated at least seven. It ended. Finally. And Peaches came out. Ferocious, confident, sexy, fearless. Barely clad in tight pink underwear and a black bra. There were dildos swinging, protruding out of the backup dancers' crotches as "Shake Yer Dix" began. Spicy, gyrating queerness all around.

> Girls and boys they want it all
> Lay back and make the call
> You need that flip, yeah really quick
> And keep it so slow it sick
> You gotta shake yer dix and yer tits
> I'll be me and you be you
> Shake yer dix and shake yer tits
> And let me be you, too

Sweat, smoke machines, cocks and tits . . . the show excelled, but more than halfway through, Peaches's face narrowed, bending over partially, a soft sway, as if she might lose her balance. A concern fell over the crowd. She leaned forward, resting her hands on her knees, head down, she began to dry heave. The music stopped. Stumbling to the end of the stage, she projectile vomited blood, spewing it all over the audience. Music back on, everyone screamed. I had fake blood all over me. My hands in the air, Peaches grabbed my elbow and ran her hand up to my wrist, smearing the red along my arm.

She was radically herself in a way that not many people are, or at least not many people in my life had been. Being as shy as I was at the time, I was in awe of her ability to be so raw and bare. She was unapologetically sexual, bold, and aggressive, her work instilled with moments of beautiful vulnerability. I only wished to be that confident and liberated, to lose the dread that held me back.

Electrified, Mark and I skipped the streetcar and walked west along Queen, the 5.2 kilometers home. The "blood" on my forearm glinted under the streetlights, we stared at it, relishing the artifact as we bounced down the sidewalk. She was still with us, that show was still with us, the queerest thing I had ever seen, that possible world. I did not want to lose that. I would cherish the relic.

I showered with my arm sticking out through the side of the curtain. It was winter, and I would be wearing long sleeves anyway. I kept it for almost two weeks. For a sixteen-year-old trans kid, she offered something that I could not find elsewhere. A voice that said, *fuck shame, fuck gender stereotypes, fuck not embracing your desires, and fuck not owning yourself.*

Altered by the concert, it wasn't just the fake blood I took home, but also a sense of discovery. I'd been in a new dimension where I'd touched my queerness, where I'd jumped and flailed in a crowd with people like me. A space for celebration, not ridicule.

I remember walking out the doors after the concert ended and a woman with a half-shaved head asking us, "How old are you guys?"

"Sixteen and fifteen," we said. Hyper and exhilarated.

"Right on," she exclaimed, seeming so proud and happy. Like all was right in the world.

Taking a deep breath, exhaling down to my toes, I wanted to hold on to the feeling, to pocket the joy, the fleeting moments of self-love. Marching home with Mark in the cold I felt the soles of my feet pressing the ground, one foot then the other. I sensed I was heading in the right direction.

Acknowledgments

———

Thank you to all the people who have helped me on my way to feeling present and alive enough to write this book. A special thank you to Julia Sanderson, who modeled queerness for me when I was younger and has stuck by me year after year. I wouldn't have been able to write this, or be here at all, without your endless love and support. To my incredible editor, Bryn Clark, thank you for believing in me and this book and making it a reality. I don't know how I got so lucky. My editor in the UK, Bobby Mostyn-Owen, thank you for your brilliance, insight, and heart. My agents at UTA, Albert Lee and Pilar Queen, thank you for thinking this possible before I did, for pushing me and making me make the time. Thank you to Meredith Miller and Zoe Nelson for all of your hard work and passion. Thank you to my manager Kelly Bush Novak for being on this journey with me, for all you've done and continue to do. Thank you to Courtenay Barrett, Amanda Pelletier, and all at IDPR. Thank you, Kevin Yorn, for always having my back. Thank you to my health-care providers, I wouldn't be typing this right now if it weren't for you and your care. Thank you to my friends who I reached out to while writing this book, for all of your guidance and support—Thomas Page Mc-bee, Chase Strangio, Lauren Matheson, Kiersey Clemons, Madisyn Ritland, Mark Rendall, Star Amerasu, Nick Adams, Paula Robbins, Brit Marling, Marin Ireland, Cazzie David, Kate Mara, Ian Daniel, Catherine Keener, and Beatrice Brown. To my mom—I love you with all my heart, thank you for being so understanding and open, you truly inspire me. To all those who have created space in this world for me to exist, well, I don't have enough words to express how fortunate I feel. This book yes, but really this newfound strength, joy, and connection is because of countless people, some I know and others I've never met. All of us on our winding paths, all of us in this together, I am grateful to be here with you.

Credits
